PRAEGER WORLD OF ART SERIES

THE HIGH
RENAISSANCE

THE HIGH RENAISSANCE

Linda Murray

FREDERICK A. PRAEGER, Publishers
NEW YORK · WASHINGTON

BOOKS THAT MATTER

PUBLISHED IN THE UNITED STATES OF AMERICA IN 1967
BY FREDERICK A. PRAEGER, INC., PUBLISHERS
111 FOURTH AVENUE, NEW YORK. N. Y. 10003
ALL RIGHTS RESERVED

© THAMES AND HUDSON 1967 IN LONDON, ENGLAND
LIBRARY OF CONGRESS CATALOG NO. 67-18404
PRINTED IN ITALY

Contents

For my Mother

CHAPTER ONE

The New Century

If a diligent search be made for the watershed between the Early and the High Renaissance – that moment when the culmination of the first becomes the point of departure of the second – then surely it must be found in Leonardo da Vinci's *Last Supper* (*Pls. 1,2*). Here, for the first time, the playful artifices of so many cherries to each place, of little dogs begging, of a Christ displaced from his central position to allow for an intrusive corbel in the architectural setting of the picture, of a Judas marked out by singularity of position, lighting, or features, of elegant observers masquerading as servants, of virtuoso still-life painting in displays of victuals and rich vessels, are completely rejected. The great picture at the end of the refectory in S. Maria delle Grazie in Milan is now a noble ruin, ravaged by time, by the results of the artist's faulty technique, by restoration and by the accidents of war, but enough survives to show that what Leonardo sought to portray was the impact upon the very different personalities of the apostles of the revelation of the coming betrayal and the presence among them of a betrayer. The picture does not, as do other, earlier, representations, set before us a narrative account of a Passover meal, but is the outward expression of the inward drama of recognition: recognition of the import of the moment, of the fulfillment of prophecy, of the nature of Christ, the consequences of their belief; that they were no longer involved merely in a sectarian argument with a purely local significance, but were present at the birth of a new conception of the meaning and nature of God which was to shatter the fabric of their lives and bring most of them face to face with violent death. Incredulity, acceptance, horror, protest, resignation, bewilderment, all are portrayed in the groups ranged on either side of Christ, who waits for the tumult to subside before continuing to speak.

7

1 LEONARDO DA VINCI *The Last Supper*

This was not Leonardo's first attempt at the portrayal of general
rather than particular aspects of humanity. The *Adoration of the
Kings*, which he had left unfinished in Florence in 1481 when he
went to Milan, contained in the figures of the Magi and their
followers characterizations of the various ages of man and the
states of mind that were associated, ideally, with them: eagerness
and vitality in the youthful, decisive faith in the vigorous, the
pathos of grateful and unquestioning belief in the aged. The seeds
even of this division – the momentary from the eternal, the ideal,
the spiritual from the material – lay in his very earliest works, for
his angels always expressed the extra dimension of the Divine, his
Virgins were the personifications of a supranormal state of woman-
hood. His ability to use nature to express the non-natural, to tran-
scend reality so as to render the immaterial, to generalize, synthetize,
so as to give a precise form to a state of mind or soul, is inherent
in all his works, even in his portraits. The great divide between
the Louvre *Virgin of the Rocks* and the later London version lies
in just that difference between the attitude of the Early Renaissance
and that of the sixteenth century, so that the Louvre picture has
much of the naïve wonder and excitement of a genius able to render

8

2 LEONARDO DA VINCI *The Last Supper* (detail)

every aspect of natural objects and to do justice to an imaginative idealization of nature in the Virgin, the Angel and the two Children, where the London picture uses a much more considered, deliberate, and intellectual idealization to give adequate expression to supernatural states of being.

Once the distinction had been made, then the rest followed almost inevitably. The new viewpoint did not conquer overnight, because the ideas that it expressed demanded a different kind of vision and ability, but it was recognized and accepted overnight, and from that moment Leonardo clarified the future role of art, and in particular of religious art. The change in style which it involved was set slowly in train, and was certain to supplant the intensely personal, more fragmented, more naïvely poetic, accidental and endearing features of Early Renaissance art.

There was another factor as well, which contributed powerfully to the acceptance of the ideas implicit in Leonardo's art. One
of the less attractive aspects of Florentine art from the 1460s onwards
was the increasing vehemence, violence even, of expression. Pollaiuolo's strained poses and exaggerated muscularity, Ghirlandaio's
insistence on the minutiae of representation, Botticelli's mounting
tension in movement and expression, Filippino's fantastic over-
elaboration, Verrocchio's heightened naturalism, forced the tone
of Florentine art to a curiously high-pitched resonance in the later
half of the century. The dissonant voice was Perugino's. His Umbrian training, outside the fevered atmosphere of Florence, led him
to create large, simple forms, with few figures, reticent in gesture
and slightly vacant in expression, carefully related to each other in
an ordered calm. Perugino, in the late 1460s and early 1470s, worked
in Florence in Verrocchio's workshop, when Leonardo was also
there, and, in the early 1480s, worked in Rome with most of the
major Florentine painters on the commission for the fresco decoration of the Sistine Chapel. Despite the powerful example of his
very different style, few Florentines were induced to abandon the
strident overemphasis of their manner; but it would seem reasonable to believe that the young Leonardo did profit by the contact.
When Leonardo came to express the most violent of emotions and
actions in the *Battle of Anghiari* (*Pl. 3*), where violence is inherent in
the subject, he expresses a quintessence of violence, a kind of idealized
and epitomized violence, rather than a detailed enumeration of
separate violent gestures and expressions. He applied to this extreme
of movement and strain the same principles of analysis and synthesis
that he applied to a static group; he knits his warriors into a single
mass of struggling men and horses with the same studied science
that he uses for the creation of a block of closely related figures
such as those in the *St Anne Cartoon*. From the first there is in
Leonardo's paintings a self-control and discipline even more taut
than Perugino's, but which the Umbrian's example must have done
much to encourage. Restraint was to become one of the most
striking features of High Renaissance art: sober gestures, carefully
controlled *contrapposto*, calm expressions, placid draperies, un-
hurried pace, accompany and underline the generalizations of form,
the idealizations of nature.

3 RUBENS after LEONARDO *Battle of Anghiari*

In 1500, Leonardo, then forty-eight, returned to Florence after the collapse of his Milanese patron's power, and with more or less lengthy intermissions he stayed in Florence until he returned to a Milan under French domination in 1506. In 1501, after making his reputation in Rome, the twenty-six year old Michelangelo returned to Florence where he was to remain until 1505. Verrocchio and Ghirlandaio had long been dead; Botticelli, though still alive, had sunk into oblivion; Perugino had retired to Perugia, there to decline into repetitive nonentity; Signorelli had dropped out of the Florentine field when he had gone to Orvieto in 1499 to paint the huge cycle of the End of the World; the Pollaiuolo brothers had gone to Rome to make Papal tombs in the 1490s and had both died there; Piero di Cosimo was active in Florence, but was never a force to be reckoned with, since his art was uncertain and the artist distinctly eccentric; Filippino was to die in 1504. The most considerable artist of the day was Fra Bartolommeo, who had been a promising painter before he became a Dominican friar after the Savonarola storm had swept over Florence at the turn of the century, and who was to rise in 1504 to become head of the S. Marco workshop, a position that Fra Angelico had once held. Fra Bartolommeo's art also expressed a serenity and repose stemming from Perugino, but with a strong strain of sentimental religiosity, and with a studied generalization of forms, features, draperies, gestures and poses, dedicated to the didactic purposes of church art, which, if it owed anything to Leonardo's example – and it probably did – was closer to an unconscious caricature than to an imitation.

It was into this world full of a vivid and recent past, and pregnant with new and potent ideas and examples, that the young Raphael arrived in 1504 at the age of twenty-one. He had been trained in Perugino's placid and spacious style, though he brought to the rather empty figures of his master's inspiration a clearer draughtsmanship and a firmer grasp of character. Nevertheless, he must have realized that if he were to compete with the Florentines on anything like equal terms, their rigorous drawing and sculptural sense of form would have to be learned. He came determined to learn them, and succeeded so well that he eventually supplanted them as the criterion by which draughtsmanship is assessed. Though Raphael spent the years from about 1504 to 1508 working on commissions in various places in central Italy, he was probably in Florence for fairly long visits. Possessed of a marvellously intuitive and ratiocinative intelligence, he analysed and absorbed from the art around him those things which had made it more vital, more interesting, more intellectually satisfying than the art of any other period since antiquity. The simple workshop formulae of triangular composition, perspective, naturalism, meaningful gesture and expression, grace, the interplay of setting, colour, light and shadow, all these he examined anew in the context of Florentine thought and practice, and his enquiring mind sorted the results into perfectly solved experiments which could themselves be used as a basis for further experiments. This is clear if his pre-Florentine works are compared with those done under the

5 RAPHAEL *Ansidei Madonna* 1505-7

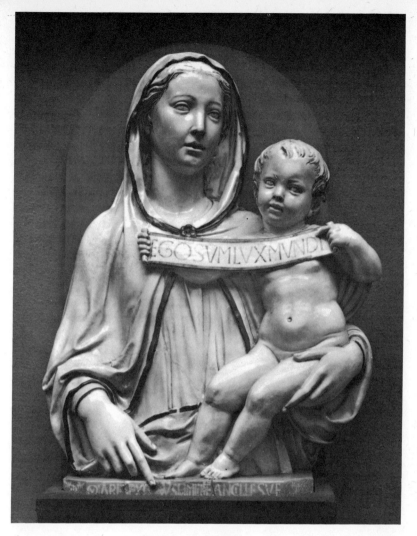

6 LUCA DELLA ROBBIA *Madonna and Child*

impact of the new inspiration: the *Mond Crucifixion* of about 1503 (*Pl.* 4) shows his typically Umbrian use of decorative flourishes in the floating ribbons, the little angels each perched upon its tiny triangle of cloud, the placid expressions of sorrow, the rather flaccid elegance of poses; the *Ansidei Madonna* (*Pl.* 5) of, probably,

1505 (the date could be read as 1507, but 1505 is stylistically more likely) shows the point from which he developed Perugino's architectural setting, and the mild expressions of his gently pious Madonnas and Saints. It is customary to dismiss the della Robbias, as if Luca, in turning from serious competition with Donatello as a sculptor in order to develop his successful enterprise as a maker of glazed terracotta reliefs, had also abandoned serious thinking for more superficial notions contaminated by money-making. But even a cursory look at many of the Madonna and Child plaques made by the della Robbia workshop will suffice to show that the revolt against the increasing complexity of late Quattrocento Florentine detail started there long before the arrival of Perugino – probably because the technique itself demanded simple forms and an uncluttered surface (*Pl. 6*). This lesson was not lost either.

The developments adumbrated by Leonardo – pyramidal rather than triangular compositions, the grouping of several figures in a meaningful relationship, the background of landscape or of shadow darkness, the contrasts of soft modelling, the enquiry into form, the idealization of nature to express the Divine – all these Raphael experimented with in the series of small Madonna and Child compositions of the type of the *Granduca Madonna*, the *Belle Jardinière* (*Pl. 10*), and the *Madonna with the Goldfinch* or *in a Meadow*. The problems presented by the interplay between the personality and appearance of a sitter, and the slight idealization, the aggrandisement of nature, demanded by the very concept of portraiture, were considered in the portraits of Angelo and Maddalena Doni, and these too stem from Leonardo so closely that the female portrait is almost an imitation of the Mona Lisa. The representation of movement, stress, emotion, coherence between figures in a dramatic context was taken up from Mantegna and Michelangelo and elaborated in the Borghese *Entombment* (*Pls. 7, 8*). The general composition is derived from Mantegna's engraving of the *Entombment* (*Pl. 9*), which also inspired Michelangelo. In Raphael's version, the seated woman turning to catch the fainting Madonna is Michelangelo's Madonna in the *Doni Tondo* of the *Holy Family* (*Pl. 26*) swivelled still further round; the figure of St John carrying Christ's legs is adapted from Michelangelo's unfinished *Entombment* now in the National Gallery, London; while the figure

7 RAPHAEL *Entombment* (detail)

8 RAPHAEL *Entombment c.* 1507

of Christ is so close to Michelangelo's *Pietà* (*Pl. 23*) in St Peter's that a knowledge of this group in Florence can be deduced from it. Michelangelo's marble roundel of the *Madonna and Child* (*Pl. 31*) with the infant St John grasping a bird, itself a motif used by

Leonardo, reappears in Raphael's *Bridgewater Madonna* (*Pl. 11*), where the sprawling Child is derived from Michelangelo, and the Virgin's *contrapposto*, her sweet smile, and the shadowed background from Leonardo.

In the late 1480s the custom of portraying figures in religious pictures dressed in contemporary costume began to give way to an increasing use of enveloping draperies of a timeless and fashionless type. At first the two continued to be mingled, as they had been from the Trecento onwards: the 1481 fresco decoration on the walls of the Sistine Chapel, Ghirlandaio's frescoes in the choir of S. Maria Novella in Florence finished in the 1490s, Botticelli's

9 MANTEGNA *Entombment* (engraving)

10 RAPHAEL *La Belle Jardinière c.* 1507

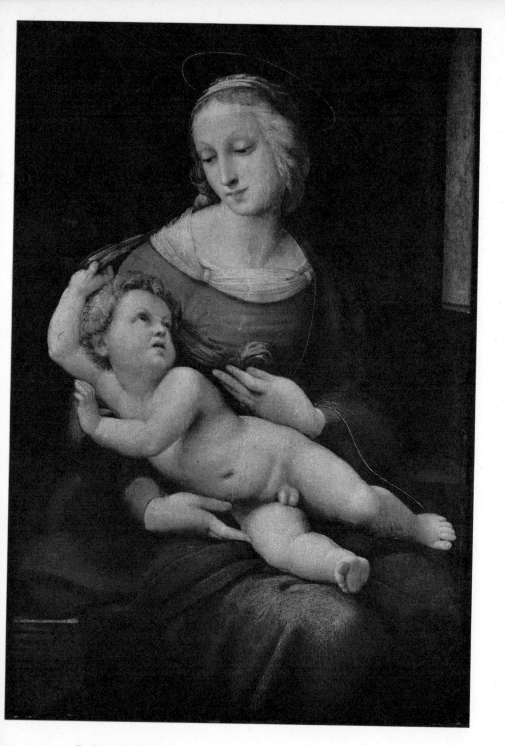

11 RAPHAEL *Bridgewater Madonna c.* 1505

late *Adorations* are examples. Leonardo never does it; Perugino only rarely, for such figures as Tobias, St Michael in armour, or saints in religious habit. Raphael compromises in his early works, for instance in the *Marriage of the Virgin* (*Lo Sposalizio*: Brera) of 1504, but once he had been subjected to Florentine influence he abandoned the practice for good.

In this he was certainly helped by the example of Fra Bartolommeo, who also rejected the mixture of the timeless and the contemporary, and in all his works pursued, with a sometimes aggressive insensitivity, a conventionalized rendering which has little in common with the kind of heightened idealization of nature that inspired Leonardo. At his best Fra Bartolommeo could achieve a noble simplicity, tenderness and sweetness; his compositions are straightforward, carefully symmetrical or pyramidal, his essays on the Leonardesque theme of the closely knit group of figures, linked emotionally, are of great beauty and pathos. Where he fails to please, it is usually through striving too much: the feeling in his grand altarpieces is often inflated, their didactic piety is too vehement, the figures are too conscious of their roles, and, like poor actors, exaggerate in sentiment and gesture, while the billowing draperies and the relentless *contrapposto* are mechanically contrived. But he was clearly one of the important formative influences on the young Raphael, just as he himself was inspired by the man he influenced. In 1508 Fra Bartolommeo visited Venice and after this his colour became more tender, his art mellower; but by this time Raphael had left for Rome, and when in 1514 or 1515 Fra Bartolommeo visited Rome the current of influence was then running in an entirely opposite direction, for the artistic centre of gravity had shifted from Florence to Rome, and Florence was never to regain its former preponderant position. In the last decade of his life – he died in 1517 – he had first the layman Mariotto Albertinelli as a partner from 1508 to 1511 in the monastery workshop, and later another monk, Fra Paolino. Albertinelli was an artist of ability and charm, but was sufficiently discouraged by the difficulties of art-to abandon it for innkeeping; Fra Paolino was a nonentity under whom the workshop dwindled into insignificance. (*Pls. 12, 13*)

Raphael was born in Urbino in 1483; Bramante in a village just ouside in 1444. Whether there was a family connection between

2 FRA BARTOLOMMEO *Mystic Marriage of St Catherine* 1512

13 FRA BARTOLOMMEO *Madonna and Child with St Anne and the Baptist* 1516

them is uncertain; however, it seems likely that it was Bramante who suggested that his young compatriot should come to Rome, probably towards the end of 1508, since Raphael was quite certainly employed on the décoration of the new papal apartments in the Vatican – the Stanze – early in 1509. This move to Rome brought him once again within the orbit of Michelangelo, who was in Florence during part of the time Raphael had spent there, occupied, from 1508 onwards, with painting the ceiling of the Sistine Chapel, a commission which, to his disgust, he found himself saddled with instead of being allowed to continue with the work for which he had originally been summoned to Rome. This was the tomb which Pope Julius II planned to have made for himself during his own lifetime. It appears from surviving accounts that there was no love lost between Michelangelo and Bramante, and fairly soon Raphael himself seems to have been involved in the hostility, as is evidenced by Michelangelo's sour remark that 'all he knows he learnt from me'.

Bramante started life as a painter, developing out of Piero della Francesca and Mantegna, whose pupil he probably was. His earliest known works are some fragments of a fresco representing a sage in an architectural setting, still in the Palazzo del Podestà, Bergamo, painted in 1477, and some rather more considerable fragments of a fresco cycle once in the Casa Panigarola in Milan, and now in the Brera. These were probably painted in the 1480s, and consist of figures, well over life-size, standing in niches, together with a pair of half-length figures of Democritus and Heraclitus with a globe between them: a cycle, in other words, based on the popular type representing Worthies. They are bright in colour, illusionistic in perspective, bold in handling. There is also a celebrated engraving (*Pl. 14*) so rare now that only two copies are known, but which must have had considerable currency in its day, since borrowings from it are found from Germany to Spain. It is inscribed as by Bramante in Milan, is datable 1481, and depicts a number of mysterious figures in a semi-ruined building, the architecture of which depends in some measure on the chapel-like setting of Piero's *Madonna and Child with Federigo Montefeltro* (*c.* 1475: Milan, Brera), only in Bramante's version the building is much larger and far more complicated. He is next found building a church adjoining the

14 BRAMANTE *Architecture
with figures* 1481

tiny ninth-century church of S. Satiro (*Pl. 15*). This building, apparently his first work in architecture, contains a *tour-de-force*, in
that from the centre of the nave the altar appears to be in a deep
choir, with a coffered vault above and shallow niches between pilasters on either side. Above the crossing formed by wide transepts
is a coffered dome. In fact, this apparently cruciform church is
T-shaped, since a street runs immediately outside the east wall of
the transepts, leaving no space at all for the choir, which is a perspective illusion only a few feet deep, an illusion which deceives
perfectly from the nave. The niches in the east wall of the transepts,

15 BRAMANTE S. Maria
presso S. Satiro, Milan
(interior)

16 BRAMANTE Baptistery
of S. Maria presso S.
Satiro

with a shell filling the rounded upper portion, the treatment of cornices, of the piers with applied pilasters that support the nave and transept arcades, of the coffering of the dome and the barrel vaults, again recall austere, Piero-inspired, classical forms. The specifically Milanese element is in the profusion of ornament which covers the forms and does its best to obscure their purity and exactness. This passion for ornament, characteristic of Milanese art (it is, perhaps the most striking aspect of the famous fifteenth-century Certosa of Pavia, where it reaches the proportions of a *horror vacui*), is particularly vivid in the little octagonal baptistery (*Pl. 16*) tucked

17 BRAMANTE Plan and section of S. Maria delle Grazie, Milan

18 BRAMANTE S. Maria
delle Grazie (interior)

into the angle of the nave and south transept. Here, the pilasters,
bent round the angles of the octagon, are covered with a delicate
tracery of relief ornament, the terracotta frieze above the varied
capitals consists of high-relief putti supporting roundels from which
project free-standing heads, and in the upper storey the pedestals,
pilasters and frieze of the piers are covered with the same kind of
profuse arabesque and foliage decorations as those in the lower
part, so that the simplicity of the plan, with four deep niches extending and moulding the interior space of the octagon, is almost
lost under layers of ornament.

During the 1490s Bramante was employed to build the east
end of the church of S. Maria delle Grazie, which had recently been
completed (*Pls. 17, 18*). Here he develops an architecture concerned with space and volume, rather than with the scenographic qual-

ities that had governed his design at S. Maria presso S. Satiro. The carefully proportioned spaces grow one out of the other; a hemispherical dome over the great cube of the main choir, with a proportionate cube surmounted by another hemisphere backed by a semi-domed niche, and the body of the main choir extended at the sides by deep semi-circular niches, the whole design articulated by a broad, strong cornice. Small windows at the base of the dome flood the interior with light. One can, of course, endlessly conjecture the influence that Leonardo, then painting the *Last Supper* in the refectory of the monastery, exercized on Bramante. The existence among Leonardo's notebooks of a mass of architectural drawings concerned with designs for centrally planned, domed churches suggests that this problem was one that both men were experimenting with, though the character of Leonardo's little drawings suggests, not that he was creating architectural designs, but rather that he was concerned with the expression of three-dimensional problems on paper, so that the solutions might be easily understood.

In 1499, the French, invading Italy for the second time, conquered Milan. The Sforza ruler, Ludovico il Moro, was captured and eventually spent the remainder of his life in a French prison. Leonardo took refuge in Venice, both from the Milanese disaster and from the attempts at patronage of Isabella d'Este, his former patron's sister-in-law, before he returned to Florence in 1500. Bramante went to Rome.

The family of Michelangelo, who were of the lesser nobility, at first opposed his desire to become an artist, and though he himself said later that he absorbed a love of sculpture with the milk of his wet-nurse, a stone-cutter's wife, he was eventually apprenticed for three years in the workshop of the important and fashionable Florentine painter Domenico Ghirlandaio. This was in 1488, when the splendid fresco-cycle in the choir of S. Maria Novella was the painter's main concern; Michelangelo was then thirteen. In years to come, he repudiated this period of formal schooling, and maintained that his genius was untutored, God-given, but it seems probable that he acquired a knowledge of fresco technique – of which Ghirlandaio was a great master – and that he made the

30

20 MICHELANGELO *Battle of the Centaurs c.* 1492

drawings that still exist after the frescoes of Giotto and Masaccio, then regarded as basic training for a pupil.

Very soon, however, he appears to have been allowed to transfer to a sculpture studio run by Bertoldo, who had once been one of Donatello's assistants, and who was now, as an old man, keeper of the Medici collection of fragments of antique sculpture, which was kept in a garden near the monastery of S. Marco. Two reliefs are the earliest works attributed to the young sculptor; the *Madonna of the Steps* (*Pl. 19*), in which the brooding

32

figure of the Virgin is placed in profile against a staircase with figures modelled in very low relief, and the *Battle of the Centaurs* (*Pls. 20, 21*), a tightly knit mass of struggling nude figures. Both probably have their origins in antique art; great subtlety in low relief was a characteristic of Donatello's art and Bertoldo is known to have been passionately interested in Roman sculpture. At the same time, the sources of classical inspiration available to the young Michelangelo included not only the classical fragments in the Garden, but antique cameos, of which there were many in the Medici collection, and these exploit the infinite gradations of modelling in delicate superimposed layers. When Bertoldo died in 1491, Michelangelo appears to have stayed on and to have been a familiar

21 MICHELANGELO *Battle of the Centaurs* (detail)

of the Medici household, but this incipient patronage came to a brusque conclusion with the death of Lorenzo de' Medici in 1492, and the expulsion of the Medici family from Florence when Savonarola came to power. During the period of much confusion and little opportunity that ensued, the young Michelangelo seems to have occupied himself with carving a crucifix, identified with one now in Casa Buonarroti, and a *Hercules*, of which the only record is in a crude print by Israel Silvestre made in 1649 showing it standing in the garden of the palace at Fontainebleau: a Hercules, a classical mythological figure, despite the fulminations of Savonarola against pagan frivolities and nudities. Then, suddenly, the French armies advancing victoriously, or at least unopposed, were at the gates of Florence, and Michelangelo perhaps feeling himself compromised by his Medici associations, prudently removed to Venice, and then, closer at hand, to Bologna.

There he made, between 1494 and '95, two small free-standing figures for the Shrine of St Dominic in S. Petronio, and one of the pair of angel candelabra for the altar of the chapel (*Pl. 22*). Clearly, he had been looking at S. Petronio's major masterpiece, the great portal carved by Jacopo della Quercia nearly sixty years before. He adapted the older master's directness of characterization, his admirable economy of gesture which concentrates the impact of the figure, and also the use of bulky draperies to give mass and weight, with a plethora of small, thick folds to indicate the form and movement of the limbs; this is also a device used by Cosimo Tura, and, though ultimately Donatellesque, it is used by both artists in a totally unFlorentine manner. There is also the strengthening of Michelangelo's feeling for *gravitas*, for the angel has nothing in common with the playful, spritely little figures found on Florentine Quattrocento tombs. He is a classically inspired, wholly supernatural being, whose dignity is a reproof to his earlier companion.

In 1496, he arrived in Rome, where he had been preceded by a small statue of a *Sleeping Cupid*, sold to an unscrupulous Roman dealer who passed it off as an antique. His first Roman patrons were the banker Jacopo Galli, and a French Cardinal, Jean Bilhères de Lagraulas. Galli bought the *Bacchus* (*Pl. 24*) rejected by its first commissioner – a life-sized figure of a smooth, plump,

22 MICHELANGELO *Angel* for the Shrine of St Dominic 1494-5

vacant-faced young man, tottering light-headedly, wine-cup in hand. The anatomy and characterization are perfect; the technique supreme; at twenty-one he has no more to learn from anyone. For the Cardinal he made the *Pietà* (*Pl. 23*), now in St Peter's. This is the final solution to the problem, which had long beset the artists of the Early Renaissance, of how to place the body of an adult

23 MICHELANGELO *Pietà* 1498-9

24 MICHELANGELO *Bacchus* 1496-7

man across the knees of a woman; it is also the unsurpassed expression of the resigned acceptance of suffering, of the acquiescence of the Divine will in the sacrifice, of God's surrender of Himself to be martyred by man. Technically, it is Michelangelo's most meticulously finished sculpture. No part but is completed to the last stroke of the chisel and polished to a high refinement of surface. The lessons learned from Quercia's use of draperies, from Leonardo's grouping of figures in a meaningful relationship, are combined with an understanding of the necessity for a timeless, unlocalized dress and for the evolution of an ideal beauty expressive of both the Divine and the human – an artistic form which shall be the equivalent of that Limbo between the Cross and the Resurrection. The forms of the heads are a trifle thin, but admirably defined and sensitive, with small, tensely flaring nostrils, sharply cut lips, and strongly marked lower lids. These contrast with the substantial modelling of the hands, the sense of the dead weight of Christ's body sagging heavily between His mother's knees, the arrested movement of the dangling legs. This is the new century's rendering of the theme so poignantly stated in the little predella panel of the *Pietà* painted by Ercole de' Roberti in the late 1480s, forming part of an altarpiece later completed for S. Giovanni in Monte in Bologna. Where Ercole de' Roberti stretches Christ's dead body rigidly across the Virgin's knees, Michelangelo bends and twists it into a measured *contrapposto* which softens the starkness without rendering it less pathetic. It is also important that the *Pietà* was commissioned by a Northerner, for the subject itself was a Northern idea, linked with German and French devotional themes of the Suffering Christ popular since medieval times in the North; there was, in fact just such a German carved group of the *Pietà* in S. Petronio.

He returned to Florence, preceded by his fame, in 1501, and during the next four years worked on a number of commissions, not all of which came to fruition. The gigantic *David* (*Pl. 25*), symbolic of the prized Florentine civic virtue of Fortitude, was envisaged as a gangling adolescent, full of the pride of youth and strength, but with something also of its uncertainty, its faroucheness, and in this differed considerably from the more urbane self-confidence of the *Davids* by Donatello and Verrocchio. The idea-

39

26 MICHELANGELO *Holy Family* (*Doni Tondo*) 1503-4

27 MICHELANGELO *Entombment c.* 1504

lization of the head is allied to an astonishing accuracy of anatomical detail in the body. The relaxed pose, with its strong links with antiquity, also expresses the medieval concept of the different affinities of the two sides of the body: the right side closed and defended against attack, the left side open and exposed, vulnerable to evil. The block from which Michelangelo carved the figure had been started on by Agostino di Duccio in 1464, but abandoned; only from the side is one aware that the imposing breadth lacks a corresponding depth, so that his achievement was a *tour-de-force*. The final position of the *David* was chosen with great care, since the

28 MICHELANGELO *Battle of Cascina* (copy by Bastiano da San Gallo)

figure has so strong a frontality, and its site – next to the main door of the Palazzo della Signoria – was selected not only to enhance the statue, but also to replace the Donatello *Judith*, taken by the City from the Medici at the time of their expulsion, and placed originally in front of the palace with an inscription celebrating the victory of courage and energy over tyranny (it was then removed to the Loggia dei Lanzi). These political overtones were fundamental to the impact made by the *David* on the Florentine public; Vasari, for instance, comments on this aspect of the *David* as a symbol of good government.

Experiments in panel painting in tempera included the *tondo* of the *Holy Family* (*Pl. 26*) painted for the patron Angelo Doni, who also employed Raphael, the *Entombment* (*Pl. 27*) and the *Madonna and Child with Angels* (both London, National Gallery), both unfinished. The *Entombment* leans heavily on Mantegna's engraving; the *Madonna* has been spoilt by other hands. His lack of perseverance suggests that already Michelangelo had formed the opinion he later expressed – that oil painting was fit only for women and the lazy. The *Holy Family* is like a relief in paint, with a hard clarity and a dazzling accuracy of drawing in difficult foreshortened poses. The Madonna's elbow and right knee mark the extreme front limit of the 'block'; the background consists of figures of nude youths – not the prophetic Old Dispensation, but unheeding antiquity with its worship of male virility, upon which the linking figure of the young Baptist turns his back as he moves towards the different plane of existence of the New Dispensation. Here, the God-Child, borne by an adoring woman and protected by an old man, uplifted as conqueror and King upon the shoulders of his ancestry, proclaims the spiritual message of the New Law, its utter separation from the Old, and the gulf between Sacred and Profane Love. Two marble reliefs are the parallel in sculpture to the *Holy Family*. Both are unfinished, as if Michelangelo had already discovered the charm of a fully finished fragment emerging from the roughly sketched-out block, like an aria soaring above an orchestral background.

29 MICHELANGELO *Drawing of a Man* (study for *Battle of Cascina*) 1504-5

The *St Matthew*, struggling to free himself from the block, was the only one of the twelve apostles ordered in 1503 for the Cathedral to be even partially completed. This was probably because work was interrupted by the commission, given in the autumn of 1504, to paint a battle scene for the Palazzo della Signoria as a companion piece to Leonardo's *Battle of Anghiari*, ordered in May, 1504. This grand project came to nothing: the cartoon was finished – at least in part – by February 1505, but the urgent summons from Pope Julius II prevented Michelangelo from continuing with the work, for which only some drawings survive (*Pl. 29*). But the impact of the cartoon for the *Battle of Cascina* (*Pl. 28*) was such that it became the main source of study for the next generation of artists, thereby emphasizing in a practical manner Michelangelo's tacit argument that only the male nude, in poses of energetic movement, was the proper subject for the artist, and the most expressive if not the only vehicle of artistic thought.

The *Madonna and Child* now in Bruges was the only other completed group of this period (*Pl. 30*). Deliberately harking back to the hieratic forms of Byzantine and medieval iconography, Michelangelo represents the Child standing between His mother's knees and enveloped in her robe, expressing both His divine and His human nature in an almost literal rendering of the ideas 'born of the Virgin Mary', and 'the Word was made flesh'. This work, just under life-size and highly finished with the same care and refinement as the *Pietà*, was crated and shipped to Flanders immediately it was finished, so that it was almost unknown in Florence. Michelangelo's letters to his father from Rome in 1505 give careful instructions about its despatch. For in March 1505, Julius II sent for Michelangelo and commissioned a grandiose tomb to be set up in St Peter's. This was the work which Michelangelo never finally completed, and which he called the tragedy of his life.

The works of this first decade of Michelangelo's career have one characteristic in common: they all show the artist affronting a technical, an artistic, problem. The earliest known work, the *Madonna of the Steps* (*Pl. 19*), is concerned with the creation of a real world of considerable spatial depth, in terms of the lowest possible relief. The *Battle of the Centaurs* (*Pls. 20, 21*) first shows him confronting his major theme: nude figures in violent action;

it contrasts with the Madonna in being in very high relief, some figures being almost free-standing. In the Bolognese works he explores problems of characterization; the *Bacchus* (*Pl. 24*) is a life-size free-standing nude; the *Pietà* (*Pl. 23*) a tightly knit group; the *David* (*Pl. 25*) is a technical triumph won in the teeth of the problems presented by its size and its having to be cut from a botched block, besides its qualities of surface modelling, anatomy, and its complex inner meaning. The *Battle of Cascina* (*Pl. 28*), abortive though it may have been and through no fault of his, was Michelangelo's first large scale painting, using the theme of the virile nude; the *Doni Tondo* (*Pl. 26*), his only finished panel painting, explores the problems of composing a meaningful group within a circle, with a precise definition of the spatial planes and relationships within the picture space, and the two marble *tondi* adumbrate similar problems in reliefs. The Bruges *Madonna* (*Pl. 30*) is a modern restatement of an old theme, which restores the hieratic quality of the subject by turning away from the sweetness, the sentimentality, by which recent sculptors had diminished its significance.

An appreciation of significance is basic to an understanding of High Renaissance art; certainly it is more complex in the variety of meanings which it presents. The medieval and Early Renaissance directness of symbolism is now replaced by multi-layers of meaning, each of which adds to the richness of intellectual content in the work. This accounts for certain difficulties, such as the confusing variety of interpretations offered quite plausibly for a large work, particularly when no written programme has survived to settle problems of exact meaning (such survivals are, in fact, extremely rare). Yet this does not invalidate contradictory views, since it is not impossible – indeed, it is very likely – that the artist himself was aware of, and deliberately exploited, such complexities of interpretation as an addition to the pleasure of the discerning spectator. The *David* (*Pl. 25*) is a fairly straightforward example. The divinely inspired shepherd-boy who saved his people and became a king is the simplest level of symbolism in its use of David as an Old Testament prefiguration of Christ, but added to this are the connotations of religious strength and self-sacrifice and civic fortitude, the inspiration from antiquity and from medieval moral apologetics in form and pose, the equation of David and Hercules as expressions

31 MICHELANGELO
Taddei Tondo 1505-6

of heroic virtue in religious history and classical mythology.
This ever-expanding world of inner meaning was understood and
highly prized by those for whom these works were made, and as
time went on deliberate complexities of interpretation become a
major factor in a work of art, particularly with Mannerist art.

CHAPTER TWO

The High Renaissance in Rome

Bramante's first Roman work was a cloister built adjoining the church of S. Maria della Pace (*Pl. 33*), and an inscription on the frieze gives the date 1504 for its completion. In Milan, in one of his last works there – the Doric Cloister of S. Ambrogio – he was still using the Early Renaissance type of colonnaded loggia which derives from Brunelleschi's Foundling Hospital in Florence, or the courtyards of the Medici Palace in Florence and the ducal palace in Urbino; since he was an Urbinate, the last must have been familiar. But in this first Roman courtyard, he adopted the pier with applied pilasters to support his main arcades, using the Roman example of the unfinished courtyard of the Palazzo Venezia, a work of the 1460s inspired by antique Roman buildings such as the Theatre of Marcellus or the Colosseum. The impact of classical Roman architecture is also clear in the little Tempietto at S. Pietro in Montorio (*Pl. 32*), which was built in 1502 as a memorial or *martyrium* on the spot on the Janiculum Hill where, traditionally, St Peter was crucified. This tiny church (it holds about ten people) looks back to antique circular temples such as that at Tivoli where there is a similar arrangement of a pair of interlocked cylinders, but the inner cylinder of Bramante's little temple projects above the outer encircling colonnade to form an upper storey crowned by a hemispherical dome. Originally, the courtyard of S. Pietro in Montorio was to have been rebuilt as a circular court with the Tempietto in the centre, but this part of the project was never carried out. The very carefully worked out proportions of this little building are in terms of both the traditional root-two measurements, used here to determine the relationship of inner and outer cylinder in width and height, and total width to total height, and the mathematical relationship of 1:1 and 1:2 in the proportions of both

32 BRAMANTE Tempietto at S. Pietro in Montorio, Rome 1502

cylinders taken together. So far as can be ascertained from the only known plan of the whole project, published in Serlio's Third Book of Architecture in 1540, these systems govern the relationship of the Tempietto to the courtyard of which it should have been the centre. The original project is of interest in that it is an instance of the persistent attitude of the Italians towards architecture: the building is not considered for itself alone, however much effort and imagination may be lavished upon it; it is a part of a complex, an element in an overall scenic effect, which it may dominate, but without which it loses its most important visual function.

In 1503 Julius II was elected to the papal throne. The ten years of his reign were not only filled with the vigour and determination of his political aims; his artistic patronage was one of the facets of his policy, and it restored Rome to a position of dominance in the arts which endured until the nineteenth century. Julius II's detestation of his Borgia predecessor extended to the rooms in the Vatican decorated for Alexander by Pinturicchio on the theme of Borgia power and success, and liberally displaying the Borgia arms and device of the bull; he ordered another suite to be prepared on the floor above the Borgia Apartments, and it was these rooms that, probably on Bramante's suggestion, the young Raphael was employed to decorate.

Julius was also faced with a formidable problem in St Peter's. The basilica built by Constantine in the fourth century had been in constant use for over a thousand years; teeming thousands of pilgrims had passed through it; Huns, Vandals, Goths, and countless other invading armies had swept over it; fires, pillage, storms, earthquakes had devastated it. Efforts had been made to repair it and to enlarge it, but by the end of the fifteenth century it was obvious that the structure would no longer endure; the walls of the nave were by this time some three feet out of the true. The papal palace was also totally inadequate. The Pope's patronage was concentrated upon five projects: the rebuilding of St Peter's, and the enlargement of the Vatican by Bramante; the decoration of the new rooms in the Vatican by Raphael; the making of a splendid tomb for himself, and the decoration of the ceiling of the Sistine Chapel, by Michelangelo.

The project for the new St Peter's was certainly decided

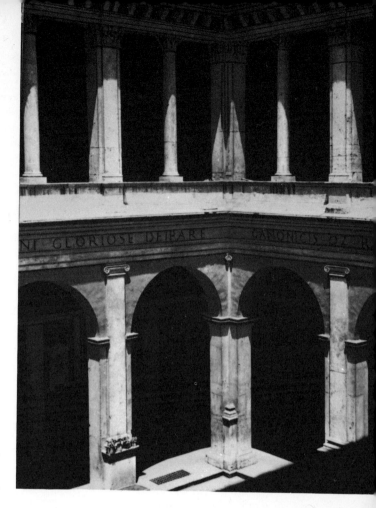

33 BRAMANTE Cloister
of S. Maria della Pace,
Rome 1504

upon by 1506, when a foundation medal was struck having on
one side a portrait of Julius II and on the other a view of the
projected new basilica *(Pl. 34)*. This was to be a centrally planned
church, based on a Greek cross, with four smaller Greek cross
elements in the angles, the central crossing surmounted by a hemi-
spherical dome borne on a colonnade. The decision to replace
a long-nave basilica with a centrally planned building must be
seen in terms of the combination of the Early Christian type of
martyrium – almost always centrally planned – with the concept
of the central plan as the expression of mathematical perfection

51

symbolizing the perfection of God. When Bramante began to work on designs for the new church he was confronted by five main problems: the position of the tomb of St Peter, which lay before the high altar, and had to become the focal point under the dome; the presence at the back of the apse of extensive foundations prepared for a new choir in the 1450s, but never completed; the restriction of the site by the presence of the Vatican buildings on one side and the requirement of continued access to the Apostle's tomb for pilgrims; the necessity of providing a benediction loggia on the façade for the great yearly papal ceremony of the blessing 'Urbis and Orbis' – the City and the World. There was also the factor that, though the dome of Florence cathedral and the choir of S. Maria delle Grazie in Milan were considerable works, nothing yet built since classical days in Italy involved construction on the scale envisaged at St Peter's. While the projects for the new church were being worked out, Bramante was already employed by Julius to reconstruct part of the Vatican, and to link the high point of the Belvedere with the rest of the palace by building a huge, elongated courtyard in rising levels, culminating in a niche on the top of the hill. Also, the main internal courtyard of the Vatican, the Cortile di S. Damaso, was started with a four-storey block on one side which showed how thoroughly Bramante had absorbed the classical heritage of ancient Rome. Tier upon tier of open arcades surmounted by an open loggia (now unfortunately all glazed in) repeat the form of the Colosseum, and established this as the most enduring type for the design of courtyards.

When Bramante died in 1514 – the year after his great patron Julius II – foundations at the new St Peter's had been prepared for the piers of the crossing and for the choir arm, but the piers upon which he proposed to erect his enormous dome were totally inadequate. All his successors progressively increased the size of these main piers and the abutments for the dome, and simplified his project. He seems to have left no detailed designs; in fact, he bequeathed to his successors the problems that had confronted him, plus the extra committment of the scale determined by the interior space of the crossing. His pupil Peruzzi, Raphael, Antonio da San Gallo the Younger, all attempted to devise solutions modifying his plans, while retaining the basic element of the centrally

34 CARADOSSO Foundation medal for St Peter's 1506. Reverse: project for St Peter's. Obverse: Julius II

planned east end. Money troubles, wars culminating in the Sack of Rome in 1527, the repercussions of the Reformation, so delayed the work that it was not until Michelangelo finally assumed direction in 1547 that any real progress was made. Bramante's great achievement lay not so much in what he actually built, but in the scale of his conception and his confidence that his ideas were capable of realization: no project was beyond the man of his age.

By 1509, Raphael was working in the Vatican on the decoration of the suite of rooms – the Stanze – designed to be used by Julius II as papal offices. The scheme of decoration is therefore a formal one with a carefully worked out programme, linking the rooms in an ordered sequence. For three rooms, Raphael was either totally or in part responsible; these open one into the next and are lit from both sides. They are cut into more or less awkwardly by doors and windows, and part of Raphael's genius was that he was able to accommodate, and even use, these interruptions, rather than to allow them to disrupt his compositions. Originally, the areas of wall below the frescoes, now decorated with a painted dado by Perino del Vaga, had *intarsie* (decorative panels of wood inlays) and probably also bookrests, but these were all destroyed by occupying soldiery after the Sack of Rome.

The room in which he began work was the middle one, the Stanza della Segnatura (*Pl. 36*), so-called because documents were sealed there. Here the theme is the divinely inspired human

53

intellect, represented by Theology, Philosophy, Poetry and Law. The room beyond it, named the Stanza dell'Eliodoro after one of the incidents portrayed, is based on the theme of Divine intervention on behalf of the Church. The first room one comes to, called the Sala dell'Incendio, also from one of the frescoes, is dedicated to miracles performed by Popes; it contains only one fresco that can claim to have any direct intervention from Raphael, as distinct from his supervision of the project. In the fourth and much larger room at the end, the Sala di Costantino, which gives on to the Loggie at the top of Bramante's new wing, are scenes from the History of Constantine and the Establishment of the Church, completed after Raphael's death by his chief assistant, Giulio Romano.

The Stanza della Segnatura was painted between 1509 and 1511, and the frescoes represent the High Renaissance at its culminating point. All the lessons of order, calm, the subordination of detail to total effect, the involvement of every part of the design in the meaning of the whole, have now been learned and are used triumphantly. The fresco representing Theology, the *Disputa* (*Pls. 37, 38*), or, more properly, 'Disputation concerning the Blessed Sacrament', must have been the first of the series to be painted. Though organized with masterly care so as to unify both halves of the composition – the celestial and the terrestrial spheres – there are certain archaisms, certain dependencies on earlier examples which suggest that Raphael was still feeling his way. The *Last Judgement* by Fra Bartolommeo, which he must have seen in S. Marco in Florence, is clearly the source for the rows of saints enthroned upon the semi-circle of clouds; the use of raised plaster for the gilded rays and bosses representing the effulgence of Heaven are ideas probably adapted from such precursors as the *Paradise* in the Signorelli frescoes in Orvieto. But these are minor aspects, of importance only in that they point the more emphatically to the break between Raphael and his predecessors. The Host exposed on the altar is the centre of the perspective of both halves of the composition; it not only unifies the whole picture in a common focus, but is also, quite naturally, the spiritual focal point of the picture, so that there is complete harmony between means and purpose. The central figures round the altar represent the Doctors

35 RAPHAEL *Portrait of Leo X and two Cardinals c. 1519*

36 RAPHAEL
Stanza della
Segnatura
1509-12

37 RAPHAEL *Disputa* 1509

of the Church; each is characterized broadly and simply, and the movement of each figure contributes not only to the pictorial movement, but also the inner meaning, just as the man with upraised arm links the two worlds physically, as well as spiritually. The movement of even peripheral figures is designed to contribute to this unity of meaning and form, to control the spectator's interest so as to direct it to the main subject mentally and visually.

The opposite wall is dedicated to Philosophy, represented by what is known as the *School of Athens (Pls. 39, 40)*. The device of the flight of steps, used in the *Disputa* to enable the swathe of figures on the earthly plane to balance those in the heavenly sphere, is a time honoured one, a modernized form of the composition of

38 RAPHAEL *Disputa* (detail)

any Trecento Coronation of the Virgin, for instance. In the
School of Athens it is the key to the composition, in that the much
steeper flight allows Raphael to compose his groups of philosophers
so that they flow into, as well as across, the picture space, and

39 RAPHAEL *School of Athens* 1509-11

permits also the construction of an architectural framework which is not only rational spatially, but is in harmony with the significance of the subject. Here, as in the *Disputa*, the placing of groups and of individual figures is done with such masterly skill that it is difficult to realize how much the eye is being directed to the focal point; at the same time, each figure is characterized so that it is not a mere compositional device, but a shorthand statement, so to speak, epitomizing the philosophical system of the figure represented. Plato and Aristotle hold the centre of the stage, the one with upraised hand pointing idealistically to a world above that of men; the other expostulates with hand spread downwards, so as to suggest the reality of the physical sciences underlying his teaching. Around them other philosophers are epitomized: Socrates, ticking off the questions on his fingers; Pythagoras with his musical scales; Ptolemy and Zoroaster the astronomers; Euclid demonstrating a mathematical problem; Heraclitus gloomily turning his back on mankind; Diogenes in rags, sprawling like a beggar on the steps. Each group is a unity, yet each group is tied to the whole by some detail that serves as a hyphen: the Socrates group by the antithesis of pose, particularly in the legs, between the philosopher and the white clad figure near him; the Pythagoras group by the still, upright young man, light against the dark profile of the figure in sharp *contrapposto* – this young man being the only upright in a succession of curves; the man walking up the steps by his position links the groups of the geometers, and by his gesture connects Diogenes in his isolation with the world about him. Through the whole of this great work there is a unity, a grasp of the construction of a design so that its complexity is concealed and all that first strikes the eye is a satisfying disposition of the parts, a feeling of order, clarity, and repose. The architecture is important in this respect; the great halls recede, high, full of light, majestic in their massive elements. The most distant point of the building, far away at the end of the transept beyond the crossing, is a light-filled arch which frames Plato and Aristotle, so that they stand out from the crowd, of which otherwise they would only be a part. This is architecture in the grand manner, the kind of thing of which Bramante must have dreamed for his new St Peter's, but never lived to build. In the far right-hand

40 RAPHAEL *Head of Plato* (detail from *School of Athens*)

corner, Raphael looks out from behind Sodoma, but to seek identities in the other figures is a waste of time, for they represent not people but formal concepts, and Raphael has listened to Alberti's warning that when portraits and ideal figures are mixed the portraits always dominate. So brilliant is his handling of the formal relationships that it is only with an effort that one recognizes here and there the source of his inspiration in a figure adapted from Leonardo or some other predecessor. But it is futile to speak of borrowings here; the personality of the painter is so overwhelming that what he borrows becomes utterly his. This is the true meaning of tradition in the arts: the absorption of ideas and their re-use for new purposes.

The *Parnassus* presented less straightforward problems – the fresco is badly cut into by the window and in his endeavour to overcome this intrusion into his picture space, Raphael has constructed a complicated composition around it, and into depth, so as to suggest that the window embrasure is behind rather than in the midst of the fresco. Perhaps the most beautiful part of the theme is the roundel of *Poetry* in the ceiling, above the fresco (*Pls. 41, 42*). The scenes representing Law are divided between three fields: two scenes representing the establishment of civil and canon codes, and, above the window, *The Judicial Virtues*: personifications of Fortitude, Truth and Prudence, figures full of movement and grace, seen in sharp perspective from below and in poses of strong *contrapposto*.

Raphael appears to have started on the Stanza dell'Eliodoro in 1511, before the Segnatura was finished. He made the larger compositions easier for himself by setting their base lines higher on the wall, so that the doors no longer cut into the picture space, and by means of painted proscenium arches, made more illusionistic by cast shadows, he set the frescoes more deeply into the wall. They are very different indeed from those in the Segnatura. The subjects are highly dramatic, as befits the theme of miraculous preservation; the content is matched by a far more energetic use of light and shadow, and by the portrayal of figures in violent movement. The completion of the first part of Michelangelo's Sistine Ceiling in 1510 was not without repercussions on Raphael's art (as, for instance, in the *Judicial Virtues*) and the vehemence of certain passages in the Stanza dell'Eliodoro suggests that here again he was prepared to adapt another man's ideas to his own purposes. The unity prevailing in the *School of Athens* is patent; that which governs the *Expulsion of Heliodorus* (*Pl. 47*) is of a more subtle kind. The story is taken from II Maccabees 3, which tells how Heliodorus was sent to rob the temple at Jerusalem of treasure which included monies held in trust for widows and orphans, and how at the prayer of the High Priest Onias a heavenly horseman and two angel warriors appeared and fell upon him, so that he was defeated in his wicked purpose. The key to the composition is the still figure of the High Priest, praying for deliverance before an altar in the temple. Like the two balances of a scale pivoting on this figure is the group of Heliodorus, violently overcome by his heavenly assailants, and that of Julius II borne by his attendants on a litter, with, in front of him, the group of widows and orphans preserved by the efficacy of the High Priest's prayer. The High Priest does not see his prayer being answered; Julius looks towards the lone figure at the altar, not at the violent struggle going on in front of him. Three different worlds are combined here: an incident in biblical history; its contemporary counterpart, in the reference to Julius's struggle against the French invaders; and the spiritual aspect of miraculous deliverance present to both, linking it with the other scenes. Stylistically, the composition hinges on the figure of the High Priest, and the union of the two sides is by a subtle counterpoint of masses and contrasting movements. Alberti's warning against the mixture of living and ideal persons has here been flouted more openly than in the *School of Athens*, though Raphael minimizes the contrasts by placing the Pope in profile, like a classical coin, and by deliberately idealizing the heads of the bearers.

The *Mass of Bolsena* (*Pls. 44, 45*) portrays the miraculous effusion of blood from the Host lying on the corporal before a priest who doubted the transubstantiation, and this miracle was popularly, though wrongly, believed to have been the cause of the institution of the feast of Corpus Christi in the mid-thirteenth century. Julius II had a particular devotion to this miracle, since it epitomized for him Divine intervention for the justification of faith, and the vindication of the Church against the vacillation of doubters and

41 RAPHAEL *Poetry Roundel* 1509

the onslaughts of heresy, at a moment when fundamental articles
of belief were being questioned. Artistically, the division between
historical personages and ideal ones is far better managed than
in the *Heliodorus*. Raphael uses the window as a podium for the
event, and for the portrait of the kneeling Pope. The worldly
side contains some of the finest portraits he ever painted – the
wonderful Swiss Guards, and the formidable presence of the old,
bearded Pope – while the spiritual side is dominated by the moving
figure of the woman with outstretched arm, personifying faith
and adoration.

66

42 RAPHAEL Study for the figure
of *Poetry* 1509

43 RAPHAEL Drawing *c.* 1517

44 RAPHAEL *Mass of Bolsena* 1511-14

The counterpart to the miraculous delivery in the temple is the fresco of Attila repulsed from the gates of Rome by Leo I in the person of the Medici Pope Leo X, who succeeded Julius in 1513. But here the imagery is trite, and the workshop hands competent but dull, and addicted to movement and gesture for their own sake.

The finest and most imaginative fresco in the room is the *Liberation of St Peter* (*Pls. 46, 48*). It tells the story from Acts 12 of Peter's deliverance by the angel from Herod's prison: this is Divine intervention to ensure the establishment of the Church in the person of Christ's appointed successor at the most desperate moment of disruption and despair in the persecution that followed the first attempts to obey the injunction 'Go ye into the world and preach the gospel to every creature'. It is expressed almost literally as light shining miraculously out of darkness – *lux ex tenebris*. One of the unusual features is that it makes use of continuous repre-

45 RAPHAEL *The Swiss Guards*
(detail from *Mass of Bolsena*)

46 RAPHAEL *Liberation of St Peter*
(detail of pl. 48)

sentation, a narrative device common enough until the end of the fifteenth century, but one almost wholly abandoned by the High Renaissance in the interests of logic and decorum. The placing of the prison with its barred window immediately over the real window, the marvellous mixture of lighting effects – the dazzling radiance of the angel, the flaring orange torchlight of the frightened guards contrasting with the cool moonlight – are examples of Raphael's mature imagination and inventiveness unsurpassed in any other work.

The remaining room – the Stanza dell'Incendio – is so called from the fresco depicting Leo IV praying that a conflagration in the congested area outside the Vatican might be halted – practically, one might say, saving the city by the force of his invocation (*Pl. 49*). Here the execution is almost totally by the workshop, and the increasing vehemence of expression coupled with the isolated character of the individual figures, their lack of cohesion as groups, as interlocking blocks with which the composition is built up, results in a diffusion of interest fatal to the impact of the whole. There are marvellous individual figures: the group of the old man on the shoulders of the young man, commonly known as Aeneas and Anchises, from the deliberate classical parallel of their escape

48 RAPHAEL *Liberation of St Peter* 1511-14

from burning Troy; the man hanging from the wall; the splendid
water-carrier with her pitcher on her head, lineal descendant of
the classical Maenad figure striding through so many Quattrocento
pictures, basket on head and draperies fluttering behind. These
are quintessentially Raphael, but the rest is boredom. Yet the
reason for this boredom is itself important. It lies in the constant over-inflation of minor figures at the expense of the relationship
of part to part, of whole to content. Also, movement and gesture,
so satisfying and meaningful in the *School of Athens* (*Pl. 39*) because
there related to and controlled by the content, have now become
ends in themselves with the consequent debasement of the language.
Julius II's patronage of Michelangelo was at first concentrated

47 RAPHAEL *Expulsion of Heliodorus* 1511-14

49 RAPHAEL *Fire in the Borgo* 1514-17

upon the tomb which he commissioned from the sculptor in 1505 (*Pl. 50*). The artist was then working on the painting of the *Battle of Cascina* (*Pl. 28*), for which the cartoon was partly completed, but at the Pope's request the Florentine Signoria sent him to Rome in March 1505; it is significant of his already great reputation that he should be used in this way for political ends. The project for the tomb underwent so many changes that it is difficult to reconstruct all the stages of the work, but originally it was conceived as a free-standing monument, about 20 feet by 30 feet, and about 50 feet high, with a room inside containing the Pope's sarcophagus. It was designed in at least two storeys, or zones, bearing about forty over-lifesize and lifesized statues, as well as reliefs and decorative sculpture in a complicated architectural setting. One of the most difficult problems is where the tomb was going to be put; an edifice of these dimensions would have fitted ill into Old St Peter's (and at the time it was planned, projects for rebuilding the basilica were still tentative) except in the new choir projected

74

from 1450 onwards, but never developed. Alternatively, a separate building may possibly have been considered. Michelangelo spent eight months in Carrara selecting the marble, and was doing preparatory work while awaiting delivery of the blocks when, in April 1506, the Pope laid the foundation stone of Bramante's new St Peter's, which meant that his resources would have to be concentrated upon the new basilica. Michelangelo's relations with the Pope deteriorated badly; he found that he could get no payment for materials or work, nor could he obtain an audience; in obedience to the Pope's orders his servants turned the sculptor away. Michelangelo flung back to Florence in a rage of humiliation, resumed his lapsed contract with the Opera del Duomo for the series of apostles, and had partly carved the tormented figure of *St Matthew*, when Julius, equally furious over the defection of his sculptor, forced the Signoria to compel Michelangelo to appear before him in Bologna, which he had captured in August 1506 during his campaign to recover lost provinces of the papal states. Michelangelo had to sue for pardon, and when a foolish cleric attempted to excuse the artist by saying that ignorant artisans of his kind could offend unwittingly, the Pope drove out the meddler with blows.

The further history of the tomb, which the sculptor described as the tragedy of his life, was fraught with trouble. When Julius died in 1513, a new contract was made with his heirs, but succeeding popes forced him to whittle down the project so that he should work for them; also, the project was enormously expensive, and Michelangelo was embittered by accusations that he had embezzled monies paid to him on account. Furthermore, Julius's heir was the della Rovere Duke of Urbino, who sided against Leo X in the wars against the French, and in 1515 the angry Pope deposed him from his duchy, and later confiscated all his wealth. Michelangelo had to let the contract lapse while he worked for both Medici popes (Leo X and Clement VII). Further contracts were signed in 1516, 1532, and finally in 1542, and under the terms of this last one a mutilated version of the original scheme was erected in Julius's titular church, S. Pietro in Vincoli in Rome, in 1545 (*Pl. 50*). The first plans for a free-standing monument were abandoned in favour of a wall-tomb – that is, a project which combined Imperial

51 MICHELANGELO *Moses c.* 1515-16

50 MICHELANGELO Tomb of Julius II

classical with Gothic precedent was abandoned in favour of a restatement of the traditional Florentine type of tomb. Only the titanic figure of *Moses* (*Pl. 51*), surviving from the 1513 contract, gives any idea of the superhuman grandeur of the original conception, which was also to include a series of figures representing the states of the soul, now known as the *Slaves* (*Pl. 52, 53*). Two unfinished ones of 1513 are in the Louvre, and four barely roughed out in their blocks are now in the Accademia in Florence, having once been used in the grotto in the Boboli gardens of the Pitti Palace: these were part of the work done under the 1516 contract. The original scheme also projected Victories, of which the large group of *Victory* now in the Palazzo della Signoria was the only one executed, and this also under the 1516 contract, though it was made while he was working on the Medici Chapel (*Pl. 117*). Finally, as the project contracted, room was only found for the great *Moses*, and for two figures of *Leah* and *Rachel*, representing the Active and Contemplative Life; a recumbent effigy of the dead Pope, and a *Virgin and Child*, flanked by a prophet and a sibyl, were executed by pupils and assistants and form the upper zone.

One of Michelangelo's characteristics was that any work on which he was intermittently engaged was always modified in the direction of whatever major work he had on hand at the time. This accounts for the strong 'family likeness' between the *Moses* and the prophets *Jeremiah* and *Joel* in the Sistine Ceiling; between the architecture of the monument and the architectural framework in the Ceiling; between the later development of the tomb design, and the tombs in the Medici Chapel in Florence. The commission for the ceiling of the Sistine Chapel was forced on him, rather than given, in 1508, more or less as a substitute for the tomb, and he accepted it unwillingly, resentfully, complaining that he was a sculptor not a painter. The first projects were for something rather simple – an illusionistic architectural structure with twelve figures of apostles enthroned in it. But as he began to work, the project grew under his hand until it developed into a cycle containing the most complicated perspective systems, hundreds of figures, a wealth of elaborate decorative detail, based on the richest, deepest and most thoughtful programme that has ever been devised. The programme itself, in a literary form, has not come

78

down to us, which has permitted the most varied interpretations, but this is another instance of the multi-layers of meaning which the work was intended to have, and which it quite easily sustains. His disappointment over the fresco in Florence and over the tomb was worked off by adapting the figures which he had mentally – and sometimes in drawings – created for them, but had hitherto been unable to use. The imagination which had been stimulated to the highest pitch of creativeness by his two abortive commissions now had a field large enough and important enough in which to deploy to the full – the only trouble was that it was not the opportunity he wanted (*Pl. 54*).

The ceiling of the Sistine Chapel is a shallow barrel vault, about 118 feet long by 46 feet wide, with windows in both long sides which cut into the vault so as to produce a series of pendentives between the windows, which are surrounded by lunettes, and have triangular shaped areas, called spandrels, above them at the junction of wall and ceiling. The central part of the vault is almost flat (*Pl. 55*), and it was probably because of this that Michelangelo defined the centre by means of a painted cornice which appears to be cut by five pairs of painted ribs running from side to side. The spaces so obtained form five small and four large rectangles, and these were filled with scenes from the Old Testament. The choice of subject was conditioned by the existence of the two series of frescoes painted in 1481-82 on the lower parts of the walls; these consist of scenes from the Life of Moses and the Life of Christ, treated as parallels from the Old Law and the New. The obvious choice, therefore, was of scenes from the history of the world before the Mosaic Dispensation, beginning with the Creation. It is important to remember that the sequence of the frescoes runs from the altar to the entrance wall, whereas the order in which they were painted is the reverse, so that the most important scene, from the standpoint of iconography, – the *Primal Act of Creation*, which occupies the small rectangle immediately above the altar – was almost the last to be painted. At the opposite end, over the entrance used by the laity, the first small rectangle to be painted contains the *Drunkenness of Noah* (*Pl. 56*), symbolic of man in his lost state wholly unconscious of God, and the biblical order of the narrative is slightly adjusted, partly to enable the complex scene of

80

54 MICHELANGELO Sistine Chapel (interior)

the *Deluge* to occupy a large rectangle, and also to obtain a progressive ascent, spiritually, from the pit of man's degradation to the ultimate splendour of God. There is also a break in the narrative corresponding to the original division of the chapel by the screen and the pattern of the floor mosaic into two equal parts – a nave for the laity and a presbytery for the clergy – but the resiting of the screen in later years to make the nave smaller and the presbytery much larger has destroyed the significance of this division.

In the first project, Michelangelo had arranged that most of the actual execution should be entrusted to skilled fresco painters working under his direction. This was normal procedure, and the Raphael frescoes in the Stanze show that extensive use of highly trained assistants does not necessarily rob the original creation of imaginative force: this only happens when the direction slackens.

As the project grew in scale and scope, however, Michelangelo was not satisfied with the workmanship of his assistants and soon dismissed most of them, retaining only such help as he needed for transferring cartoons, and painting the enormous area of architectural and decorative detail. As the sixteenth century understood it, the work was his alone, and in all the major parts it is entirely by his own hand, and has come down to us very nearly intact, so that it is the first of his great paintings, and the highest point of his early maturity. From the spring of 1508 until September 1510 he worked on the first half of the Ceiling; from 1510 there was a long break during which fresh scaffolding was put up for the second half – the part nearer the altar. The first half was officially unveiled on the 15th August, 1511, and after this work proceeded so rapidly on the second half that the whole was unveiled on the 31st October, 1512. The second part is more freely painted and simpler in colour, as well as much larger in scale. This progressive increase in scale is apparent from the beginning: the Delphic Sibyl, the first of the pendentive figures, is larger than the corresponding Prophet Joel on the other side of the *Drunkenness of Noah*, and the nude youths framing the third history are larger than those framing the first. In the *Fall and Expulsion* scene, and in the *Creation of Eve*, the figures are much bigger and simpler than in the three earlier histories, and such was the enlargement that the figure of God in the *Creation of Eve*

83

55 MICHELANGELO Sistine Chapel ceiling (detail)

is so large that if He stood upright His head would be cut off by
the frame. High up on the scaffolding, Michelangelo must have
found it difficult to get a proper view of his work, though clearly
he took measures to see part of it after the third history; it was not
until the break in 1510-11 that he could examine his work critically,
and the greater breadth, and the abandon of such finicking details
as gold used in the decorative parts, is the result.

84

The most important parts of the decoration iconographically are the nine Histories, which are generally simple in subject and easily identified. For instance, the *Expulsion from Paradise* is treated in much the same traditional way that Masaccio had used nearly a century before; yet not all are so obvious in meaning, nor have all of them precedents in earlier Italian art. The *Deluge*, with the ark in the background, is plainly recognizable, but it is not a common subject – the famous Uccello in Florence is the best-known earlier example – neither is it treated in quite the same way, since it stresses not so much Divine punishment for sin, as the helplessness of man and his hopeless condition if, by abandoning God, he cuts himself off from his means of salvation. The *Creation of Eve* marks the completion of the first half of the Ceiling; the later frescoes are not only simpler and grander in style, but are also entirely new pictorial equivalents for the first verses of the Book of Genesis. The last four scenes over the choir end of the Chapel deal with the world before the Fall of Man: the *Creation of Eve* is exactly half-way – before the Fall, but the Creation of the means of the Fall. The change is evident in the *Creation of Adam*,

56 MICHELANGELO *Drunkenness of Noah* 1508-10

with its now famous symbolism of the huge and sluggish form of Adam vivified by the spark of life which seems to pass between his limply upraised hand and the outstretched, commanding finger of God. The other scenes represent the Creation of the Earth, the Sun and Moon, the Vegetable and Animal Kingdoms, with God swinging round in one vast orbital movement; but it is the last scene of all, immediately above the altar, which has always caused the most comment. This – one of the smaller fields – consists of a single figure, much less than full length, and therefore proportionately larger than the others, symbolizing God dividing light from darkness, or the creation of form from chaos (*Pl. 57*). No one before Michelangelo – and few since – have had the hardihood to imagine the beginning of things in pictorial terms, and it is a measure of the gulf which separated the Early Renaissance from the great period at the beginning of the sixteenth century that no fifteenth-century artist, not even Donatello, would have been capable of this image. But the image is not isolated, and it is in its context with the rest of the Ceiling that its true importance lies, for the Histories are linked with the figures of Prophets and Sibyls and the scenes from the Old Testament in the angles. There are seven Prophets and five Sibyls. From among a multitude of each these twelve were chosen, the men because their particular prophecies accorded with the iconography of the central field or because the tenor of their prophetic thought was in harmony with contemporary circumstance and ideas; the women because they are classical pagan equivalents of prophets, rhapsodic describers of the Creation who, from non-Jewish origins, testified to a belief in the chosen people specially favoured by God, from among whom the Redeemer should be born, not just to the Jews, but to all mankind. Each of these figures occupies the pendentive extending between the windows, level with the smaller Histories; each figure epitomizes pictorially the character of the Prophet or Sibyl chosen (*Pl. 58*). Thus the Prophet immediately above the altar is *Jonah* (*Pl. 59*) who is the accepted prefiguration of the Resurrection; this figure of Jonah leans backward in a fantastically complicated and difficult pose, so that he – the Resurrection symbol – looks up at God the Father in the Act of Creation. On either side of Jonah are large triangular spaces, made by the junction at the corner

86

of a pair of pendentives, and these contain scenes from the Old
Testament traditionally regarded as prefigurations of the Crucifixion and the Redemption of Mankind – the Crucifixion of Haman,
and Moses and the Brazen Serpent above the altar wall, David

58 MICHELANGELO Studies for the *Libyan Sibyl* 1511-12

and Judith above the entrance wall. At various points during the celebration of the Mass the priest is directed by the rubrics to raise his eyes to Heaven, and thus the celebrant at the altar in the Sistine Chapel, looking upwards, would be aware of the two symbolic representations of the Crucifixion, another of the Resurrection,

88

IONAS

and finally, and most appropriately, of the only possible pictorial equivalent for the words of invocation to the Holy Ghost. It is evident that each scene was very carefully planned and dovetailed in with the representations of the Prophets and Sibyls. Below these figures in the lowest and darkest part where the window cuts into the vault and the wall, are representations of ordinary human beings who are the Ancestors of Christ – those whose names are listed in the genealogies at the beginning of St Matthew's Gospel (*Pl. 60*). These figures, some single, some in groups, are painted with extraordinary breadth and fluency; they were probably the last to be executed, and their importance as links between the Ceiling and the wall-frescoes is often overlooked.

One important element remains. The four larger Histories occupy the entire width of the vault between the painted cornices, but the alternating five smaller Histories fill only about half the space, the remainder being taken up by large, bronze-coloured medallions painted with small symbolic scenes, now very difficult to see. The medallions are the excuse for the introduction of the celebrated nude figures of young athletes – the so-called *Ignudi* – four of whom are seated at the angles of each of the smaller fields (*Pls. 61,62*). Nineteen and one head survive – the rest of the twentieth, together with part of the sky of the *Deluge*, was destroyed by an explosion in the Castel Sant'Angelo in 1797. The real purpose of these figures is difficult to determine. It has been suggested that they represent ideal versions of the human race during the first years of Humanity; this really means that they represent the Neoplatonic idea of the ideal Man, which may be right, since Michelangelo as a young man was in contact with Neoplatonic circles in Florence, and his theological views around 1510 were not necessarily the same as those he is known to have held at the end of his life. At the opposite end of the scale, it has been suggested that Michelangelo added these figures simply because of his passion for the male nude, and that they are a continuation of the ideas that had preoccupied him during his work on the Battle cartoon. This does not explain fully their very important part in the composition, nor is it likely that Julius II – a man of strict piety and rigid decorum – would have acquiesced in the view that the Vatican Chapel was a fit place for the display of Michelangelo's

60 MICHELANGELO *Ancestors of Christ: Jacob and Joseph*

formal obsessions. From the artistic standpoint, it is clear that
the possibilities offered by these seated figures fascinated the painter;
the *Ignudi* are not controlled by the same rules of perspective as
those governing the architectural framework they inhabit, but act
as a kind of unifying element between the illusionism of the frame
and the direct frontality of the Histories, and also as an intermediary
in scale between the pendentive figures and those in the Histories.
They too participate in the general increase of scale towards the
altar, but even more significant is their diversity of pose.

   In the first two sets each pair is derived from a single cartoon
which is then reversed, so that with modifications to the lighting
each figure has a different aspect. In the second set, Michelangelo
introduced considerable changes, always in the direction of more
movement and greater complexity in the pose, so that each figure
became an independent creation. At the beginning of the work,
the use of reversed cartoons – which is done consistently for the
putti on either side of the thrones of the Prophets and Sibyls, and
under the labels at their feet, and for the shadowy figures in the

61 MICHELANGELO *Ignudo* 1508-10

62 MICHELANGELO *Ignudo* 1511-12

small spandrels on either side of the thrones – was a labour-saving device probably introduced so as to make use of assistants. But as the quality of his helpers dissatisfied him, and he undertook more and more of the work himself, only the minor decorative parts were thus simplified.

When the Ceiling was completed and unveiled, Michelangelo's dominant position – even higher than that of Raphael – was established beyond any argument. But Julius II died only a few months after the unveiling of the Sistine Ceiling, and the new Pope, Leo X, was a man totally lacking in the titanic quality of his predecessor. He was, however, a great patron of the arts. He determined to employ both Raphael and Michelangelo, but it was clear that in order to do so he would have to circumvent Michelangelo's contract for the Tomb, and also find work for him which would both occupy him fully and not be competitive with Raphael. To employ Raphael in Rome and Michelangelo in Florence was the obvious course. He had known Michelangelo since boyhood, for as the son of Lorenzo de' Medici they had the same Florentine background, but, as he later remarked despondently, 'Michelangelo is impossible to deal with'. Michelangelo's work on the Tomb was therefore cut short, and he was dispatched to Florence on a project for a façade for the family church of S. Lorenzo.

During the next years Raphael's reputation and career was in an ever-mounting ascendant. The charm of his personality is attested by all who left any record of him; no tantrums, no displays of temperament, the most perfect manners and urbanity, good humoured, convivial, with a lively appreciation of women to which Vasari, with rather envious smugness, attributed his early death. In his art, his ability was uncontested, his knowledge and understanding of antiquity deep and universally accepted by humanists and scholars such as his friend Bembo; commissions of every kind poured in on him – portraits, devotional easel pictures, religious and secular decorations, tapestry cartoons, architecture, the supervision of St Peter's after Bramante's death, the responsibility for listing and conserving the antique remains of Rome. Without a well-organized workshop he would have been lost, and it is yet another of his triumphs that his versatile and capable team achieved so much of passably good quality. In the case of Giulio

Romano, he produced an artist of the first rank whose contributions were far and away superior to those of the average studio hand. Giulio developed a style personal, influential, and quite different from that of his master, upon whom he even came to have a certain effect.

Raphael needed all these things. Though the greatness of many single works – the *Stanze*, the *Sistine Madonna* (*Pl. 67*), the portrait of Castiglione (*Pl. 66*), the *Galatea* (*Pl. 65*) – is such that he could have triumphed in any one of his spheres singly, yet the quintessential quality of Raphael is that he is greater in the sum of parts than he is in any of them individually. The range of his mind, quick and intuitive, yet profoundly thoughtful in the attitude he brought to bear upon his problems, his gift for inspired borrowing, for assimilating the best ideas of others, his sensitivity to new trends, make him the most intelligent of the great creative brains of his age. Leonardo excelled because he first identified the problems, examined them – almost, one might say, created them by isolating the factors which constituted them. Michelangelo triumphs by pure intuitive genius, by creating in his mind, not problems, but forms, ready made, needing only to be freed from the matter imprisoning them – as he himself said in one of his sonnets, 'The greatest artist never had a thought The marble block itself does not enclose Within its shell...'. Raphael is supreme because he faced the problems he had to solve, and then set about doing so with absolute certainty and confidence. He is the most deliberately intelligent of painters, because he accepted the patrons he had to work for and the limitations they imposed on him, and he understood his own strengths and weaknesses. It is, above all, the quality of his understanding, the strength of his intellect and humanity, the sublime power of his draughtsmanship, which make him the most deeply satisfying, the most inexhaustible artist of his age.

His main commissions in the next years were very varied: the decorations for Agostino Chigi, the Sienese banker who was his friend and patron, the cartoons for the tapestries designed to hang below the 1481 fresco cycle in the Sistine Chapel, numerous portraits, many inventive variations on the theme of the Madonna and Child group, a couple of palaces in Rome, and the Villa designed for

Cardinal Giulio de' Medici. His easel portraits were rarely of the formal grand-manner type: Julius II, in the Pitti, is more the sensitive reflection of an old man, wearied by his ceaseless struggles, than the proud and energetic pontiff who appears in the Stanze frescoes; Leo X and his two nephews, Cardinals Ludovico de' Rossi and Giulio de' Medici, the future Clement VII, is more an intimate and psychologically penetrating study of power and satellites. His greatest portraits were of those closest to him: the reticent, unaffected beauty who was the model for so many of his Madonnas, and whom he painted with a veil over her head, looking calmly, confidently, at the spectator; the court poets Beazzano and Navagero, intimate friends, painted as if interrupted in a conversation; his other great friend, Count Baldassare Castiglione (*Pl. 66*), an Urbinate like himself, author of 'The Courtier', preceptor of all who aspired to the conduct and manners of gentlemen. In dark clothes and simple white shirt, he looks out of the canvas calmly and dispassionately, the embodiment of his code that a gentleman wears sober colours and spotless linen, is restrained in behaviour, quiet of speech, and shows his breeding by his modesty and impeccable deportment. His artistic lineage is as grand as his hereditary honours, for Raphael has been inspired to remember the *Mona Lisa*, and the half-turned pose of head and shoulders, the clasped hands, the quiet colour and impassive expression with just a hint of movement in the mouth, prove that even as late as this – the portrait was painted about 1516 – he could still acknowledge a debt to Leonardo. It is, perhaps, pertinent to remember that Leonardo himself was possibly at this moment still resident in the Vatican, the guest of Cardinal Giulio de' Medici who hoped for great things from his patronage, but was totally disappointed, for in the three years from 1513 to the end of 1516 that Leonardo spent in Rome he was interested only in scientific problems, and not a hint of the great artistic developments taking place around him appears in any of his notebooks. Raphael's only considerable change is to substitute a plain background for Leonardo's fantastic landscape, and this change is one that accords not only with the personality of the sitter, but also with the essential stylistic differences between the first and the second decades of the century. In its turn, this portrait inspired both Rubens and Rembrandt.

96

During the years when he was working on the Stanze, Raphael continued to experiment with the Madonna and Child theme. One of his sketchbooks, the so-called 'Pink Sketchbook' now broken up and divided between a number of museums, contained little compositional ideas very like some of the Leonardo drawings which are the prelude to the *Adoration of the Kings* and the *Madonna of the Rocks*. In these sketches, the *Madonna di Foligno (Pl. 64)*, the *Bridgewater Madonna (Pl. 11)* inspired ultimately by Michelangelo's *Taddei Tondo (Pl. 31)*, the *Alba Madonna* and the *Madonna della Sedia*, to name only four, can be seen in their genesis. In general, Raphael's Roman Madonnas follow the new forms dictated by sixteenth-century theories on decorum: timeless draperies envelop the Mother of God, who appears as a Heavenly visitant to her votary on earth. The *Madonna di Foligno* shows the donor, the papal historian Sigismondo de' Conti who commissioned the picture for the high altar of the church of the Aracoeli in Rome where he intended to be buried (he died early in 1512), kneeling with his patron saints below such a vision, recalling the tradition that the church was built upon the site of an apparition of the Virgin. The Madonna is taken directly from Leonardo's *Adoration of the Kings*, and the Child is adapted from Michelangelo's *Doni Tondo (Pl. 26)*, but these deliberate borrowings are really no more now than the use of classical quotations in a new context. Unfortunately, the crude nimbus is a later restoration, and the group of saints and donor are heavily studiohanded. In the lower half, only the *putto* is authentic Raphael, brother to the tablet-bearing angels in the *Disputa (Pl. 37)*.

Raphael's most celebrated Madonna is undoubtedly the *Sistine Madonna (Pls. 67, 68)*. This famous picture has suffered so badly from its fame that it is now almost impossible to see it with a mind uncontaminated by the distortions of pietistic imagery – holy pictures, plaster statuettes, gaudy enamelled plaques, embroidered banners, the debased artistic currency of good intentions crossed with sentimental religiosity. It is not Raphael's fault that his masterpiece is so universal in its appeal, so uncomplicated in its form and meaning, so direct and tender in its emotion, that the power to see it afresh and to recognize its artistic qualities have been almost destroyed by the repellent popularity thrust upon it by over four centuries of commercial exploitation. It was used as a *velarium* – a kind of

65 RAPHAEL *Galatea c.* 1511

6 RAPHAEL *Baldassare Castiglione c.* 1516

screen – to be placed over the bier of Julius II; hence the papal crown standing on the balustrade upon which the two small angels prop themselves reflectively. Carefully placed in relation to the bier this surface would become an extension of the bier itself. Hence also the figure of St Sixtus, an Early Christian pope and martyr, adopted by the della Rovere as their family patron, wearing a cope patterned with the acorns and oak leaves of the family badge – the first della Rovere to become a pope, Julius's uncle, took the name of Sixtus IV. Hence also St Barbara, invoked against sudden death (Julius was in fact a long time dying), in whose commemorative mass the Lesson is a paean of gratitude for deliverance in war, and from calumny and sedition. The visionary aspect of the picture is stressed by the curtain running on the rail at the top, and parted so that the apparition shall appear framed in its folds over the dead Pope's coffin. The Madonna does not walk on the clouds, but is wafted forward, her cloak and veil billowing around her, serene, majestic, barefoot, not because she is a simple peasant woman, but because she carries the Godhead in her arms, and the 'ground' she walks on is holy. Sixtus looks up at her while gesturing towards the dead man he sponsors; Barbara looks down at the *putti* leaning on the bier; the movement of eye and mind travels up and down again in a coordinated process of thought, noting the frontality of the main group, where the two bodies are yet turned at right angles to each other, the compensating movements and gestures of the saints, and the way the whole is fitted together with such beautiful precision. Though Raphael pursued the theme until the end of his life, no other Madonna achieved the effortless splendour of this one.

The cartoons for the tapestries, commissioned by Leo X, were begun in 1515 and sent to Flanders to be woven in 1516; the first seven were hung in the Sistine Chapel in 1519, and received with acclaim. In subject matter, they completed the iconographical theme of the decoration of the chapel, for the Ceiling deals with the Creation and the redemptive promise made to Noah, the Prophets and Sibyls record the history of the Creation and the promises of God, the ancestors of Christ represent humanity in the expectation of redemption, the parallel Lives of Christ and Moses the two Dispensations, and the tapestries begin with the Miraculous Draught

67 RAPHAEL *Sistine Madonna c.* 1513

of Fishes and the injunction to Peter 'Feed my Sheep' – that is, with the establishment of the Church and its mission – and continue into the Acts of the Apostles with the lives of Peter and Paul, concentrating on those aspects of the apostles' careers which exemplify the Church as the means through which redemption is to be achieved. Naturally, the workshop played a large part in the execution, yet much of the designing, and possibly even of the actual handling, is by Raphael himself. For the *'Feed my Sheep' (Pl. 71)*, for example, there is an autograph drawing which shows him working

103

68 RAPHAEL *Sistine Madonna* (detail)

out the theme of the ripple of recognition and hesitation running through the group of apostles on the shore, to the telling hiatus that separates the kneeling Peter and the passionately believing John from the figure of Christ. So important is the significance of this theme that it is the only subject to appear twice in the chapel, for the tapestry echoes in several ways Perugino's fresco of the *Charge to Peter* on the wall above. In the *Miraculous Draught* (*Pl. 69*) and the '*Feed my Sheep*' the tension mounts with the flow of the action towards the still figure of Christ at one side, yet the action is contained entirely within the picture. In the *Healing of the Lame Man* the architecture of the Beautiful Gate of the Temple so threatened to overpower the miracle in the centre that a host of attendant figures was introduced to redress the balance, and some of these, in gesture and expression, or in, for instance, the musculature of the grotesquely adult child in the foreground, produce an extraordinary diffusion of effect. The two divine punishment scenes, the *Death of Ananias* (*Pl. 70*) and the *Blinding of Elymas*, are planned centrally; the *Ananias* in many ways resembles the *Heliodorus*, not only in the pose of the fallen Ananias, but also because the central motivating force is set back into the composition, and there is a distracting almsgiving

69 RAPHAEL *Head of St Peter* (detail from *Miraculous Draught of Fishes*) 1515-16

scene on the left as a counterpart to the group of Pope Julius and his litterbearers. In both these scenes, in the equally dramatic *Sacrifice at Lystra*, and in two which are known only from the tapestries themselves, the *Stoning of Stephen* and the *Conversion of St Paul*, the composition flows on outside the scene with figures lopped off in mid-career as they come, so to speak, into the focus of the artist's concern. The *St Paul preaching at Athens* combines the two types: the figure of the apostle, arms upraised but otherwise still, faces an almost motionless group; only at the sides is there a hint of movement outside the composition, in the two believers on the right and the similarly truncated forms of the doubters on the left.

The most striking artistic parallel is that in all the tapestries, except the *Miraculous Draught* and the '*Feed my Sheep*', there is an inflation of gesture, movement and expression similar to that found in the Stanze after the Segnatura. There are splendid details: the columns of the Beautiful Gate, the magnificent gesture of St Paul rending his garments, his majestic simplicity at Athens, and the fascinating architectural detail which includes, at Athens, a curious recension of the Tempietto rather clumsily altered from a rectangular building with green columns. The cartoons, of which only seven survive, remained in Flanders after the weaving was finished. There they became one of the chief vehicles for the dissemination of Italian ideas, but with the unfortunate corollary that the new style was

71 RAPHAEL 'Feed my Sheep' 1515-16

equated with the over-inflation, so that it was the superficial aspects of movement and drama that attracted the praise and imitation. These cartoons and others by his assistants were also one of the means whereby Raphael's international fame spread over Europe.

Contemporary with the tapestries are the small vaulted compartments of the Loggie, on the second floor of Bramante's range of the Cortile di S. Damaso, which Raphael completed after the architect's death in 1514. These are filled with illusionistic trellises and architectural perspectives, incorporating small biblical scenes – the so-called Bible of Raphael, finished in 1519. They are almost totally the province of the studio, but fascinating, however, in that they show, like the late Stanze, the tapestries, and the Chigi decorations, the evolution of a new style, going beyond the forms of the first years of the High Renaissance towards greater expressiveness and dynamic movement. It is unthinkable that this change in style should have been imposed on Raphael by his assistants, and if they display it with less sensitiveness than he does, it must still be because he

107

70 RAPHAEL Death of Ananias 1515-16

himself was tending that way, though perhaps with more restraint, and they over-interpreted his tendencies. There is plenty of evidence that this change of style was intimately connected with the appreciation of the antique, particularly the type of classical art represented by the Laocoon and the Apollo Belvedere – that is, with a classical art expressive of powerful emotions and consciously poetic grace. These qualities, so highly prized in the antique, became also the main qualities which the modern artist sought to express, hence the elegant rhetoric of gesture and pose, and the deliberate elaboration which, from the second decade onwards, becomes the dominant stylistic preoccupation. Coupled with this pervasive influence from important and recently discovered antiques, was the inspiration of the illusionism and use of violent foreshortenings found in the Sistine Ceiling. It can be argued that Michelangelo never ceased to influence Raphael; upon lesser talents his effect was almost wholly disruptive, because they believed that form and content could be divorced, whereas in Michelangelo they are indivisible.

For the banker Agostino Chigi, Raphael undertook two chapels, one in S. Maria della Pace, the other in S. Maria del Popolo, and the decorations in his Villa Farnesina. Again, the studio was necessarily extensively employed here, but it is astonishing how high a proportion of the planning and execution in these works is, in fact, autograph. The architecture of the chapel in S. Maria del Popolo is also his – a centrally planned building, with a compartmented dome rising to an illusionistic open 'eye', like the Pantheon,

through which can be seen a vision of God the Father accompanied
and supported by *putti* – a variation on the theme of the open dome
which Mantegna had invented in the Camera degli Sposi in Mantua over forty years earlier. In the compartments of the dome
are scenes representing the Signs of the Zodiac and the Astrolo-
gical Houses, so that God the Father, as the Creator of Heaven
and Earth, presides over Chigi's horoscope and receives the soul
that has completed its earthly cycle. The Farnesina decorations,
done between 1516 and 1517, enlarge the programme begun by
Raphael with the *Galatea* (*Pl. 65*) painted about 1511; this is a
light-hearted sparkling fresco in which the central figure of the

72 RAPHAEL *Wedding Feast of Cupid and Psyche* 1516-17

nymph is a secular version of the *Madonna di Foligno* (*Pl. 64*). With no more than seven figures, a few *putti* and some sea-beasts, he suggests a riotous, revelling crowd, speeding over the waters. In the adjoining Loggia, Raphael recreated for his friend the classical garden room, hung with garlands and roofed by tapestries stretched beneath the open sky. Here the story of *Cupid and Psyche* (*Pls. 72, 73*) unfolds itself slowly from pendentive to pendentive, culminating in the *Council of the Gods* and the *Wedding Feast* on the ceiling. The pictorial illusion of the tapestry hanging solves the problem of the perspective system of the ceiling paintings: since they pretended to be tapestries slung so as to provide a shady awning overhead, they were absolved from the need to create an illusion of space in which the figures should appear as if they were really disporting themselves among the clouds, while the pendentive figures are painted with a moderate illusionism, consistent with their being seen, as real actors in their garlanded stages, from the opposite side of the loggia.

Raphael's contribution to the designing of the new St Peter's was totally negative. There had always been opposition to Bramante's central plan: it was a difficult shape, liturgically; it did not provide enough room for processions or for large concourses; it was deficient in sacristies and subsidiary chapels; it set the façade of the church further back than the existing atrium front, and therefore wasted some of the space available which could be used to advantage inside. During Julius's lifetime his decisive personality made further protests unavailing, but Leo X was a much more easy-going man. After Bramante's death, the way was clear for the objectors, and Raphael's plan changed Bramante's project by adding the equivalent of another three bays to the easternmost arm (St Peter's has a reverse orientation). Eventually, the objectors won, for despite later returns to the central plan the final form was the present long-naved basilica – Maderno's seventeenth-century modification of Michelangelo's plan.

Raphael's own house was probably designed by Bramante (*Pl. 74*); it was a simple, five-bay, two storey block on an island site; a basement of a range of shops – the open shops of classical antiquity such as are still commonplace in Italian towns – with storage mezzanines over, built with fairly heavily rusticated blocks so as

74 BRAMANTE House of Raphael. Engraving by Lafrery

to make a strong contrast with the smooth upper storey of the *piano nobile*, where each bay had a large pedimented window with a section of balustrade below, framed in a pair of applied columns. The plain Tuscan Doric order carried an entablature concealing an attic, and a simple cornice projected over the whole. This plain, unaffected form became the standard for perfect symmetry and balance, proportion and discipline. The building was later destroyed in a street widening scheme, and it is known only from this engraving and a delicate drawing by Palladio. Raphael's own palace designs are based upon this form, but with important alterations, nearly always in the direction of added richness – more complicated rustication in the basement, a wealth of stucco relief in the *piano nobile*, with niches and swags and variations on the window pattern, so that the rigidly compartmented bay system is broken up, more light and colour is introduced, and the architecture is subjected to a process of enrichment and ornamentation similar to the search for poetic grace and movement in painting. Basically, however, the Bramante House of Raphael type, with the Colosseum type of superimposed arcade, used either separately or combined as façade and courtyard, are the basic elements of Italian palace design for the next four centuries.

The Villa Madama is the reconstruction of another antique form: the country villa, close to the city, designed as a house for pleasure and recreation. Cardinal Giulio de' Medici commissioned it, but hardly lived in it, since Raphael died when it was little more than started, and in 1527 it was badly damaged during the Sack of Rome. Its remains were later restored for Margaret of Austria, 'Madama' or senior lady of the Austrian Imperial house. In the original project, a huge villa was designed round a circular court-yard, with a splendid open loggia (*Pl. 75*) giving on to magnificent terraced gardens stretching across the top of Monte Mario, then just outside Rome; only one wing was partly built, but this is one of Raphael's most influential works, since the form of the loggia, articulated by a Giant Order and with huge open bays and superb stucco decoration, was the model for many that came after. The stuccoes were based on grotesques and arabesques, with tendrils sprouting from slender vases, fan-shaped bat-wing mouldings, little sphinxes, cameos and medallions of late classical decoration, and the painted vaults repeat these themes with even greater richness and fantasy; their inspiration was the recently excavated Golden House of Nero, so that they offered an irresistible combination of the charm of novelty with the re-use of a classical type. The decoration in this loggia forms the greatest possible contrast to the little church of Sant'Eligio degli Orefici, the chapel of the Goldsmiths' Guild, built soon after 1509, almost certainly in association with Bramante. It is a domed Greek cross, of great purity and sparseness, with no or-nament but its fine-drawn lines and a beautifully lettered inscription round the eye of the dome. But this bare, mathematical beauty, dependent on harmony of proportion, was soon found to be lacking in the excitement, in that learned quality present in the element of quotation, which adaptation of late classical decorative forms provided; the bare walls and empty volumes of pure form were then clothed in ornament, so that the same transitions can be found in Raphael's architecture from the beginning to the end of the decade of his Roman career as can be found in his paintings.

In 1517, Cardinal Giulio de' Medici, who was Archbishop of Narbonne, commissioned two altarpieces for his cathedral; one was the *Raising of Lazarus* from Sebastiano del Piombo (now in the National Gallery), the other was the *Transfiguration* from Raphael

75 RAPHAEL Loggia of the Villa Madama, Rome

76 RAPHAEL *Study of heads of two Apostles and of their hands c. 1517*

(*Pls. 77, 78*). The scene is taken almost literally from Matthew 17, where the account of the Transfiguration is immediately followed by the story of the healing of the possessed boy, yet these two entirely separate incidents are conflated by the wide pointing gestures of the disciples in the lower part, who seem to be trying to make the screaming boy see the vision. The contrast between the divine radiance of the vision and earthly confusion and sorrow, between the means of salvation in which one must believe rather than just witness, and the blindness and suffering of unregenerate human nature, made insensible of its state by possession by sin, seems to be the programme behind this work, and this conflict and tension is stressed by every means in the painter's power. This

77 RAPHAEL *Transfiguration* 1517-20

ambivalence must have been intended by Raphael from the start, since some of his most beautiful drawings are studies for the heads of the apostles in the group in the centre of the crowd (*Pl. 76*). In this, his last work, exhibited in an unfinished state over his bier at his funeral, and yet sufficiently far advanced to be so shown, Raphael is clearly moving towards a phase of his art characterized by mounting emotion and movement, vehemence and dramatic effect. The completion of the work was by his assistants, who may have stressed the new forcefulness at the expense of serenity and balance; but it is clear that this work was a new departure, long meditated in the later Stanze and the tapestries, but which his untimely and sudden death on Good Friday, 1520, left to be exploited by his successors.

78 RAPHAEL *Transfiguration* (detail)

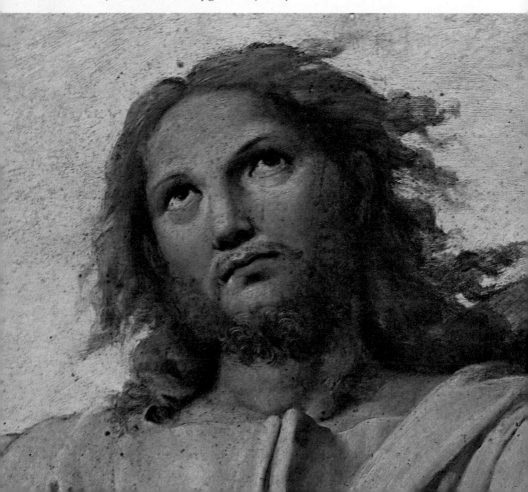

CHAPTER THREE

The High Renaissance in Venice

In his life of Giorgione, Vasari makes two illuminating remarks. He says that Giorgione was deeply influenced by Leonardo and imitated Leonardo's soft and tender modelling; and he extends his comments by saying that Giorgione's imitation of nature rivalled that of Tuscans who were creating the modern style. He gives to Giorgione in Venice the same position that he gave to Leonardo in Florence in that he equates him with the creation of a new style, a modern style, which superseded that of Bellini and all his other predecessors and contemporaries. The comment on the imitation of Leonardo has usually been dismissed as another instance of Vasari's Florentinism – his determination to make all the best in art anywhere derive from a Florentine example. Yet it is not as improbable as it at first appears. Leonardo was actually in Venice, though only for a matter of weeks, in 1500 after he left Milan. His stay, however short, was not without leaving a deep impression behind, since in 1505 Dürer, in Venice for a visit, took up the theme of *Christ among the Doctors*, which Leonardo had been asked to paint by Isabella d'Este, and had evaded doing. Dürer's picture is so Leonardesque that it may seriously be suggested that some work, possibly a cartoon, by him was in Venice, and that in this self-sufficient city he was known by more than mere hearsay. In 1500, Giorgione would have been in his early twenties – he is said to have been born at Castelfranco, some thirty miles north west of Venice, about 1477/8, and to have been brought up in Venice as a pupil of Giovanni Bellini. He is recorded in the State archives in 1508 as receiving payments for an unidentified picture; he is known to have painted frescoes on the outside of the newly rebuilt Fondaco dei Tedeschi (the northern merchants' warehouse) in 1508; he died in 1510, for on the 25th October Isabella d'Este wrote to her agent in Venice instructing him to obtain a 'Night' (which usually means a Nativity) from among his effects. He replied that Giorgione had recently died of plague, but that no such picture was in his estate; he had painted two, but neither owner would sell. On the back of a portrait now in Vienna, called *Laura* (*Pl. 79*) from the laurel leaves surrounding her head, is a label saying that it was painted on the 1st June 1506 by Giorgione. For a major painter, founder of a new style with far-reaching repercussions on the art of a whole region, it is almost the least amount of documentation known. There are, also, the notebooks of a Venetian connoisseur, Marcantonio Michiel, who recorded pictures he saw in the houses of Venetian notabilities between 1525 and 1543. He records fifteen works by Giorgione, but of these only three can be positively identified, and of the three, two, he states, were finished by others.

The *Three Philosophers* (*Pl. 82*) finished by Sebastiano del Piombo, the sleeping *Venus* (*Pl. 83*) finished by Titian, and the *Tempest* (*Pl. 81*) mentioned by Michiel, the *Laura*, a surviving battered fragment of the Fondaco frescoes, and the *Madonna and Child with Sts Francis and Liberale* in the cathedral at Castelfranco (*Pl. 80*), which has never been questioned although the earliest mention of it is in 1648, are the core of the attributions to him. There are no signed works, nothing documented but the Fondaco frescoes. The field is enlarged by the two unknown *Nativities* mentioned by Isabella d'Este's agent, and a handful of ill-defined portraits and other subjects listed by Michiel. Yet the canon of accepted works is rather larger because, basically, Giorgione's style, as it can be defined from the hard core, is unmistakable; confusions with Titian occur, particularly in works from early in Titian's career, because Titian himself contributed to the confusion by completing works left unfinished in 1510, and because he was himself so deeply involved with Giorgione's new style.

The Castelfranco *Madonna* (*Pl. 80*) can be seen as a grand-manner *sacra conversazione* of the type begun in the 1470s by Piero's *Madonna* in the Brera, and the Venetian ones by Antonello and Bellini in the 1470s and 1480s, though by comparison with Bellini's great altarpieces it is quite a small picture, less than seven feet high and smaller even than the Piero. It is also part of the gentler, more tender tradition of Bellini's smaller devotional Madonnas set in a landscape.

79 GIORGIONE *Laura* 1506

The Madonna has a distant, thoughtful, dreamy air, the Child lies passively in her lap, the two saints look neither at her nor at each other, but out at the spectator. The St Francis is a quotation, in reverse, from Bellini's St Francis in the S. Giobbe Altarpiece, yet nothing could be more different than these two works. Its proportions are extraordinary: the Madonna is enthroned high upon an enormous pedestal, so high indeed that the two saints' heads are well below the bottom of her throne, so that one is tempted to wonder whether Giorgione did not modify his composition from one in which the Madonna was seated originally upon the lower part of the pedestal where the beautiful brocade now hangs. The landscape is entirely in the upper half, and the saints are excluded from it by the high wall at the back of the throne; it is as serenely peaceful as any landscape in one of Bellini's late Madonnas. The light is undramatic, flowing softly round the figures, casting only the slightest of shadows and enhancing the mood of tender, reflective

81 GIORGIONE *Tempest*

GIORGIONE *Madonna and Child with Sts Francis and Liberale*

piety. While the separation of the Madonna from the world of the saints and the scene outside fits the change in feeling current in the early Cinquecento in Madonna pictures outside Venice, yet she and the Child are so close to Bellini's elegiac vision that only the physical separation of earthly and divine, and the personal appeal of the saints to the spectator, mark this as a sixteenth-century picture.

The *Tempest (Pl. 81)* is a mystery. No one, not even Michiel, who mentions it as early as 1530, has ever suggested a plausible subject; he records it merely as 'a small landscape... with the storm, and the gipsy and soldier...'. Was there ever a precise subject? It is doubtful, since X-rays have revealed the ghost of another nude woman under the soldier's feet, which would suggest that Giorgione painted it as a landscape of mood, and added figures according to fancy. As a landscape of mood, however, it stands supreme. In the sultry heat, the woman suckles the child, with a kind of pensive tenderness as if she were an earthly form of Madonna with a purely human baby; a curious by-stander (why a soldier? He bears no arms, for his staff is not a lance. Only his slashed breeches suggest a *Landsknecht* – a German mercenary) watches her, and in the distance, beyond the little town to which the bridge leads, a storm has broken and rages furiously. Yet no hint of wind or even a ripple of breeze has reached the detached pair in the foreground. Does it represent the Elements: earth, water, air, and the lightning for fire? Or the Senses: sight, sound (presumably there is thunder in the lightning), touch, taste – but where is smell unless it is implied by the rosebush? Or does it represent Nature: man, woman and child, with the elements around them, and the architecture and his dress to suggest the intellect of man contrasted with her nudity as Nature elemental and unsophisticated? If the answer were known it would be just the answer to a puzzle; it would neither add nor detract from the picture, for its secret has little to do with its magic.

The *Three Philosophers (Pl. 87)* has been badly cut down on the left: an old copy shows much more of the rock, on which Michiel comments in 1525: '... with the rock imitated so marvellously...'. The subject again is a mystery. Are they the Magi? The Three Ages of Man? The Active, the Contemplative, the Enquiring Mind? The Philosophies of Greece, the East and of Rome or the Middle

Ages? Why did Giorgione alter the old man's head-covering from a diadem to a cowl, and does it have any bearing on the subject? What is certain is that upon this work, and ones like it, is based the argument that Giorgione's heightened perception of nature is what brings him into Leonardo's orbit. Bellini's *Stigmatization of St Francis* of the 1480s also has a minute approach to nature in its elaborate detailing of rocks, plants, animals, distant hills and town, and yet no one could call it Leonardesque; the difference between them, therefore, must be in their approach to nature. The Bellini is episodic, the forms assembled and juxtaposed rather like pieces in an exhibit; while the picture is full of marvels they are, somehow, individual marvels brought into a slightly artificial unity because it is essential for the religious content that St Francis should be adoring the works of his Creator. In the Giorgione, the parts of

83 GIORGIONE *Venus*

the landscape and the figures cohere; there is no violation of scale between the shelving steps of the rock and the men or the plants; the atmosphere envelops them all equally. As in Leonardo's *Virgin of the Rocks*, nature and humanity are one creation, different in kind but not in essence. The *Venus* (*Pl. 83*) expresses the same feeling. Michiel says '...nude Venus, sleeping in a landscape with Cupid... but the landscape and Cupid were finished by Titian'. X-rays show that the Cupid is under the landscape at Venus's feet, so that this part of the picture must have been finished by Titian and repainted at some time after 1525. Nude figures were no longer, at this date, a rarity, but she is astonishingly unusual. Her peaceful sleep divorces her entirely from the spectator's world, and there is none of that self-consciousness later found in Titian's *Venus of Urbino* (*Pl. 97*).

Attributions to Giorgione depend, as a rule, on four things. The atmosphere: there must be this feeling of common mood in man and nature, this almost mystical quality found in the Castel-franco *Madonna* or the *Venus*. The colour: Vasari, who wrote about Giorgione after visiting Venice and consulting people who had known him (Titian, for example), remarks in the Life of Sebastiano del Piombo that Giorgione introduced into Venice 'a harmonized manner, and a certain brilliance of colour'. There must be an emotional quality in the colour, a richness, a vibrancy, memorable as much in the modelling and the transitions of greys or creams as in passages of brilliant colour. The content: this is rarely straight-forward; there must be a hint of mystery, a withdrawal from overt characterization, for instance in portraits, and in fancy subjects the equivocation becomes complete. Even in religious pictures (for instance, in the Prado *Madonna and Child with Saints* attributed to him, but probably partly by Titian) there is the detached, absent quality found in the Castelfranco *Madonna*. The actual forms: Giorgione's heads tend to be round with firmly rounded chins, straight noses and short upper lips; the compact, slightly plebeian features of Laura recur frequently. Even the Castelfranco *Madonna*

84 GIORGIONE *Concert Champêtre*

and the *Venus* have this type, though in both these cases rather more idealized than, say, in the *Tempest*, the Oxford *Madonna*, or the Madonna in the Allendale *Adoration* (Washington).

What of the problem pictures? The *Shepherd Boy* at Hampton Court, the *Young Man* in Berlin (*Pl. 85*), the Louvre *Concert Champêtre* (*Pl. 84*), the *Woman taken in Adultery* (Glasgow), the *Concert* (Pitti), the *Judith* (Hermitage), are the main ones, and there is also a group of male portraits, particularly of men in armour, and a number of small landscapes with figures, usually a classical story or myth. The Berlin portrait is universally accepted; the *Shepherd Boy* is accepted as a very damaged original: both have the sensitive tenderness and the delicacy of handling agreed as hallmarks. The *Judith* is now generally accepted; certainly it has the astonishing flaming colour, the sensitive withdrawal, the deliberate abstention from the more sensational aspects of the subject. Was this, by any chance, the painting done for the State commission? Was it a Justice subject for an official position? Is not the *Adulteress* too active, the poses too energetic, seen from too unusual a viewpoint to fit in with the mystery and restraint characterizing his other works? The colour, too, though very startling and strong, is just enough on the crude side to suggest an adventurous follower rather than the master himself. The *Concert* and the *Concert Champêtre*, so different in every way, have one thing in common: in both, two musicians turn and look into each other's faces with a yearning, hauntingly intimate glance. The haunting look is a favourite device of Titian's; most of his figure compositions, religious or secular, have it, for it is one of the ways in which he ties a composition together internally, whereas the certain Giorgiones avoid this involvement between the figures. The women in the *Concert Champêtre* have a strongly Giorgionesque character, but the landscape, and the handling of the paint and brushwork are closer to Titian. Is it a work which Giorgione had begun before his death, and which Titian completed for its commissioner?

At most, Giorgione's career can have been no more than ten years long, but it sufficed to introduce four new features into Venetian art: the secular subject, painted in small size, for private houses, private enjoyment, collectors, much as Bellini had introduced small religious works never destined for a church; tender chiaroscu-

ro, with infinitely delicate gradations of modelling, and richly evocative colour; the nude; and landscapes painted for their own sake.
In all these he not only set the style of the new century, but exercized
a powerful influence on Bellini himself. The S. Zaccaria altarpiece
of 1505, the exquisite *Madonna degli Alberetti* ('with the little trees')
of 1510 in the Brera, the *Feast of the Gods* and the *Toilet of Venus* of
his last years show how responsive the old Bellini was to the new
ideas and feeling abroad. Then there was Giorgione's impact on
the younger generation: Palma, Sebastiano, Titian, Savoldo, Paris
Bordone, and Dosso Dossi, hastened to follow in the path he first
trod. He also seems to have been the antithesis of the usual pro-
fessional painter: like Leonardo, a lover of music; like Raphael,
a lover of women (his undoing, in that he is said to have caught
the plague from his mistress); his delicate and poetic temperament
bring him clearly into the Cinquecento orbit of Raphael, for the
painter who is also a poet, a musician, a man of education and

85 GIORGIONE *Portrait of
a Young Man*

86 TITIAN 'Ariosto'. Portrait of a Man

87 TITIAN Bishop 'Baffo' presented to St Peter

breeding, besides being a genius, is an essential feature of the new century. No one exemplified the duality of the artist of the Renaissance more than Titian, who was the heir, not only to Giorgione's unfinished pictures, but to the position his untimely death left open in Venice.

Titian was born at Cadore, a hill town in Venetian territory, and sent to Venice when still a child to be trained as a painter, first in the workshop of a designer of mosaics, and then with the Bellinis. His immensely long and important career contains only one problem: his birthdate. In 1571, in a letter to Philip II of Spain, asking for overdue payment, Titian said he was 95; this makes him born in 1476. Vasari, who knew him, begins by saying that he was born in 1480 and later says that he changed from Bellini's to Giorgione's manner of painting when he was eighteen, and another mid-sixteenth century writer says that he painted frescoes at the Fondaco with Giorgione when he was twenty. This makes him born in 1488. Titian's earliest work is usually considered to be the portrait of Bishop 'Baffo' (Jacopo Pesaro, Bishop of Paphos in Cyprus) kneeling before St Peter and receiving from Pope Alexander VI the command

88 TITIAN *St Mark and the Plague Saints c. 1511*

of a papal fleet (*Pl. 87*). This took place in 1501, and Alexander died in 1503. The picture is evidence of just that change of manner to which Vasari refers, since St Peter is very Bellinesque, with tightly crumpled folds in his raspberry pink robe, while the figures of pope and bishop are more broadly and freely painted. If Vasari is right in his second dating, then Titian would have been born about 1484, and have been an assistant to Giorgione on the Fondaco when he was about twenty-four. A birthdate between 1484/88 is a more rational one, since it is difficult otherwise to account for so great a genius as Titian being merely an assistant to a man of his own age when thirty-two. In December 1510 he was in Padua, where in 1511 he painted three frescoes in the hall of the Confraternity of St Antony, and in 1513 he declined an invitation to Rome in order to return to Venice. Sebastiano had gone to Rome in 1511; this meant that, with Giorgione dead and Bellini in his eighties, Titian could expect soon to achieve an outstanding position. Bellini, in fact, lived until 1516, and Titian caballed against him relentlessly in the last years of his life in an endeavour to displace him from his official position.

There are, in Titian's continuous output of masterpieces, certain works which are like landmarks; these are the pictures which mark some new development – a new treatment of an old theme, a new solution to a standard problem, a new approach in vision or meaning, a new technical departure. Giorgione, in the years following his death, has a strong influence on Titian. The so-called *Ariosto* portrait in the National Gallery (*Pl. 86*) with its use of the little parapet to set the figure into space, the softness of the modelling, the enveloping quality of the light and that sense of air around the sitter, stems from Giorgione. The *St Mark and the Plague Saints* (*Pl. 88*), now in the church of the Salute in Venice, was painted probably as a thank-offering for the end of the terrible 1510 plague, and it has – besides its startling innovation – a sense of unity of surface, of depth in colour and composition also basically Giorgionesque; the innovation is the rather gauche device of allowing the shadow of the great columns to fall across St Mark's head and shoulders. It enables Titian to achieve an exciting design by silhouetting the saint darkly against the creamy coloured clouds, and also detaches him effectively from the group below. The superb *Sacred and Profane Love* (*Pls. 89, 90*), of about 1515 is in the direct line from Giorgione's mysterious fancy pictures – no one has so far suggested a firm subject for a work clearly of the same 'family' as the Louvre *Concert Champêtre* (*Pl. 84*); in a sense it is quite different, but this is because where Giorgione was a creature of mystery and obliquity, Titian is a direct, overt personality. His nudes are never diffident, and his pensive woman here is quite decided in her attitude. The small *Madonna and Child* in Vienna, known as the 'Gipsy Madonna', is clearly in the direct line from Bellini's late ones; but with the lovely Madonna groups of the years immediately after Giorgione's death (Edinburgh, London, Madrid, Dresden, Genoa) a new line is opened up. These are barely larger than the late Bellini Madonnas, but the feeling in them is of much more movement, the forms are fuller, and the composition depends on a more complex balance and rhythm of poses. The colour is

89 TITIAN *Sacred and Profane Love c. 1515*

more richly modulated, and the sweet and tender Madonna has given place to a more opulent, grander type of female beauty. The same process is at work in his portraits of women: Giorgione's rather shy Laura is succeeded by superb beauties, like the Louvre *Girl doing her Hair*, or the same girl posing as *Flora* (*Pl. 91*), or as *Salome* (Rome, Doria Gallery). Whether true or fancy portraits is irrelevant; what matters is the new type of picture, for they are collectors' pictures, bought because paintings are now things to possess and admire and are not merely objects or stimulants of piety. Even the old Bellini understood this new current, for the *Feast of the Gods* and the *Toilet of Venus* painted in the last years of his life exploit this secular vein, just as he understood the import of Giorgione's new withdrawn approach to the Madonna picture, as his late *St Jerome* altarpiece in S. Giovanni Crisostomo shows.

With the *Assumption of the Virgin* (*Pls. 93, 94*), in the Frari, Venice, a new stage is opened. The commission was given in 1516, and the picture unveiled over the High Altar in 1518. It is a huge work, about 23 by 11 feet, half as large again as Bellini's biggest picture. The composition depends upon the surge of the figures, for here the Virgin is not merely rising into Heaven: she is virtually projected upwards by the compressed force emanating from the compact group around her empty tomb, and is poised against the radiance of golden light suffusing the sky behind her. The new attitude towards representations of the Virgin is very obvious here; like Raphael's *Sistine Madonna* (*Pl. 67*), with which it is contemporary, this is

132

90 TITIAN *Sacred and Profane Love* (detail)

91 TITIAN *Flora c.* 1515

no merely mortal woman, but the Mother of God, human in her rather timid and adoring confidence, yet aware of her glorious destiny. Just as Raphael in the *Disputa* (*Pl. 37*) had used one man's gesture to link the earthly and heavenly spheres, so Titian uses the same device, and the astonished apostle is the earthly link, as the little angel beneath the heavy load of his cloud is the heavenly link with the earthly zone. The handling of the light and shadow pushes the silhouette device tried out in the early *Plague Saints* (*Pl. 88*) much further. There is, throughout, a brilliant use of a rich texture of light, woven in and out of the composition, and obeying the logic of the movement, so that the apostles stand amazed in the shadow cast by the skein of angels tumbling about on the clouds which accompany rather than support the Virgin as she soars from darkness towards the source of light.

After this, nothing can astonish. The *putti* from the *Assumption*, as well as their heavenly role, also play in an infant *Bacchanal* round the feet of Venus, and flutter like little plump birds among the trees. This and the *Bacchanal of the Andrians*, were painted between 1518/19 for Alfonso d'Este, Duke of Ferrara, for his '*studiolo*', for which the London *Bacchus and Ariadne* (*Pl. 92*) was painted in 1522, and the first picture in the series had been Giovanni Bellini's *Feast of the Gods*, painted in 1515, in which Titian repainted the landscape to match the other pictures in the series. The *Infant Bacchanal*, or 'Homage to Venus', and the *Andrians*, are subjects taken from descriptions by Philostratus of ancient Greek paintings; the *Bacchus and Ariadne* is from one of the several accounts of the myth, as it is told by Ovid for example. The composition of the *Infant Bacchanal* is odd, in that the focus of the design is on the extreme right, in the statue of Venus, while in the *Andrians*, despite the energetic movement from the back to the foreground of the picture, the attention is rivetted upon the superb nude in the very front. She is, of course, Titian's answer to Giorgione's Venus – sleeping, quiescent, oblivious; but her pose instead of the soft, relaxed Venus, is tense, and her nudity is a deliberate contrast with the semi-clothed figures of the other bacchantes, and almost a heightening of the effect by the implications of moral progression. As in the *Assumption*, the light moves backwards and forwards in the picture, making islands of shadow amid the brilliant sunlight, and the poses of the figures in the foreground are so arranged as to lead the eye backwards into depth. Only the splendid nude is an isolated fixed point, and in the far

2 TITIAN *Bacchus and Ariadne* 1522

93 TITIAN *Assumption of the Virgin* 1516-18

background the drunken old man on the hillock epitomizes the degrading aspects of inebriety which her beauty and peacefulness effectively disguise. The *Bacchus and Ariadne* has the same remarkable feature as Raphael's *Galatea (Pl. 65)*: with no more than seven figures Titian suggests a riotous throng pressing forward upon the startled Ariadne, while Bacchus's movement, suspended in mid-career, suggests the godlike power of levitation. Between the two main figures the distant landscape looks towards quiet villages and sea-shore, and in all the series the landscape is as important a part of the composition as the figures, and is suffused with air and light; these are not landscape backgrounds, but figures in a landscape. There are subtle quotations, too, by which Titian proves that he

94 TITIAN *Assumption of the Virgin* (detail)

knew what was happening elsewhere in Italy: from Michelangelo's *Battle of Cascina* (*Pl. 28*) in the *Andrians*, from the antique *Laocoon* in the *Bacchus*. In this group of works, painted for a discerning patron, Titian's imagination grows with his technical powers. The handling of the wonderful nude, or of the bacchante behind Bacchus, is full of tenderness in its management of light, and of the dappled effects of passing shadow. These mythologies look forward to the *Venus of Urbino* (*Pl. 97*) of 1538 – that even more deliberate challenge to Giorgione – though here he is really fighting in a different battle. This Venus is no goddess, caught unawares on a summer afternoon; this is an expensive and successful courtesan, her hair tumbling from her diadem over her creamy shoulders, her lovely face empty of all expression but that of self-confident self-admiration, displayed with the trappings of her art upon an all too suggestive bed, with her maids in the background laying aside her worldly store in rich chests while she lies contentedly, 'for where your treasure is, there will your heart be also'.

In 1526 he finished another of the turning-point pictures, not just of his own career, but of the whole history of Venetian painting: this is the *Pesaro Madonna* (*Pl. 95*) commissioned in 1519 by the same Bishop of Paphos who had been represented in the first of his major works in 1502/3. This is more a Madonna and Child with Saints and donors than a *sacra conversazione*, but one very different from all earlier ones. For the first time the composition is oblique, with the Madonna seated upon a high throne well to one side, St Peter virtually in the centre below her; the male members of the Pesaro family, kneeling on either side below, are *repoussoir* elements which push the composition back into the picture space. The device of the huge columns is also important for the future: they punctuate the composition carefully, so that the great vertical rising from the kneeling Pesaro on the right continues through the St Francis and the upright Christ Child, and the one on the left

95 TITIAN *Pesaro Madonna* 1519-26

96 After TITIAN *St Peter Martyr* (engraving by Martino Rota)

defines the back plane of the composition and accentuates the two figures leaning away from each other – St Peter inwards towards the Madonna, the standard bearer with his gorgeous banner outwards towards his captive Turk, to create a massive block above the kneeling Bishop. The sequence of the Madonna's head, the base of the column behind her, St Peter's bald head looking down and his brilliant golden robe lead across the picture down to the dark figure of 'Baffo' in his black silk gown, while at the top the columns pierce a small cloud bearing *putti* with a Cross; this device not only fills the upper part but also echoes the light and shadow below.

The next great landmark has been destroyed: his *Death of St Peter Martyr*, finished in 1530, was burnt in the same fire in SS. Giovanni e Paolo in 1867 in which the first big Bellini *sacra conversazione* was lost. The composition, known from copies and engravings (*Pl. 96*), bursts open like an explosion; the murderer and the fleeing companion form a huge open V rising from the dying saint, and the trees soar upwards and outwards to echo and reinforce this movement. In the midst of the foliage, two *putti* brandishing a martyr's palm hover as if appalled at the deed below. The novelty here is not just in the movement, but in the way the trees are made to participate in the emotion of the scene.

The *Presentation of the Virgin* (Pls. *101*, *102*), finished in 1538, and still in the place for which it was painted in what is now the Accademia in Venice, marks another stage in his career; after this, something darker, more troubled enters his art, something which, later, his stay in Rome strengthened. He was now the foremost painter in Italy after Michelangelo. Of his major Venetian competitors, Palma Vecchio was dead, Pordenone – once his friend but his inveterate rival after Titian won the public competition for the *St Peter Martyr* – was to die the following year, Sebastiano had never returned from Rome except for a visit in 1529 when Michelangelo was also in Venice during his brief flight before the siege of Florence, Lotto worked outside Venice, and people like Cariani, Romanino, Savoldo, though interesting were not really competitors at all. Titian remained supreme, and it can be contended that his position in Italy was not seriously challenged even by artists of the stature of Andrea del Sarto, Pontormo or Correggio. Only Michelangelo was of the same metal, until Tintoretto appeared on the scene. During these years, he had also become the most important portrait painter in the world: the *Young Man with a Glove* (Pl. *98*), of about 1520, full of air and space; *Federigo Gonzaga, Duke of Mantua*, perfumed and gallant, playing with his pet dog, of about 1525/28; the full-length portrait of the *Emperor Charles V* (Pl. *99*) with his mastiff, copied in 1532 from Seisenegger's similar portrait with such success that Titian immediately displaced the German as the Emperor's favourite portrait painter; the splendid pair of *Francesco Maria della Rovere, Duke of Urbino*, and his *Duchess, Eleonora Gonzaga*, which must have started as full-length portraits since Titian's drawing of the warrior-Duke shows him standing; and the group of female portraits – *Isabella d'Este*, in clothes and headdress as pretentious and with a pretty but obstinate face as meanly hard as her whole personality; the gorgeous *La Bella* (she is the courtesan who is also the *Venus of Urbino*); they became the norm by which portraiture

97 TITIAN *Venus of Urbino c.* 1538

was judged. Though he does not seem at any point to be indebted to any non-Venetian inspiration, yet the largeness and spaciousness which informs all his portraits, even the least significant, partakes of the atmosphere and understanding which is a characteristic of all Cinquecento Italian portraiture from Leonardo on. Dull though it is, since it is a spirited copy only, the *Charles V* is possibly the most important, since this full-length portrait marks a new development. Full-length portraits occur first in Germany – notably the pair by Cranach of *Henry the Pious of Saxony* and his *Duchess* of 1514 – and then spread south of the Alps with Moretto of Brescia (*Pl. 100*), who dated one in 1526, though of course the genre is inherent in donor portraits in religious works, which had only to escape from their religious context to become subjects on their own. They represent, however, a distinct stage in the esteem for

98 TITIAN *Young Man with a Glove c.* 1520

painting and collecting, and, also, in the liberation of the portrait from its earlier limitation to bust and half-length, one of great importance during the rest of the sixteenth century and during succeeding ones.

A large part of Titian's main works during the most productive part of his career consisted of official portraits of the Doge, histories and battle pieces for the adornment of the Doge's Palace, and paintings for the Doge's private chapel in the palace: all these perished together with the history paintings done from the early fifteenth century onwards by Pisanello, Gentile da Fabriano, Gentile and Giovanni Bellini, in the great fire of 1577. This loss means that almost nothing is known of the forms and style he evolved for dealing with this type of work. In 1545/6 he visited Rome, where he painted Pope Paul III and his Farnese relatives in a group which remains one of the most shattering documents about the Pope and his sycophantic family – and which remained unfinished probably for that reason. He also experienced Michelangelo's *Last Judgement,* and the great Roman works of the maturity of the High Renaissance. It would be idle to claim that he was unaffected by

99 TITIAN *Emperor Charles V with his Dog* 1532
100 (*far right*) MORETTO *Portrait of a Man* 1526

them. In, for instance, the *Martyrdom of St Lawrence* (*Pl. 103*) painted in the late 1540s, many details suggest his study of these works, from the vehemence of the figures to the different sources of light with which the picture is shot through. The series of splendid nudes – the Danäes and the Venuses of the late 1540s and the 1550s – are clearly influenced not only by Roman painting but by the great collections of antique statues in the Vatican. In 1548/49, and again in 1550/51, he visited the Imperial Court at Augsburg, to paint official portraits which set the type of such works for all court artists onwards. After the Emperor's abdication in 1555, when his Spanish dominions passed to Philip II, the Spanish king acquired a constant stream of *poesie* – as Titian himself described his mythological subjects – which included the wonderful *Diana and Callisto* on loan to Edinburgh, the *Rape of Europa* in Boston, and the later version of the Roman *Danäe*, still in the Prado. Philip also bought a large number of copies and versions of his earlier mythologies, as well as religious works, such as the second version of the *Martyrdom of St Lawrence* (*Pl. 104*) for the Escorial, and the pair of *Entombments*, poignant rethinkings of

101 TITIAN *Presentation of the Virgin* (detail)

102 TITIAN *Presentation of the Virgin* 1538

an old theme. It was this concentration by Philip upon the art of Titian that made him blind to the peculiar merits of El Greco.

Titian's art in the late years changed from the splendid optimism of his early religious pictures, and the confident serenity of his spacious portraits, into a troubled manner, in which the forms are enveloped in mystery and the colour expresses the most intense feeling. Only for a very short time was he affected by Central Italian Mannerism, which for a fleeting moment pushed him into experiments with lighting effects and strained poses. Much is known about his technique, for it was described by Palma Giovane who finished the *Pietà* (*Pl. 105*) destined by the artist for his own tomb, and not completed at his death. 'He laid in his pictures with a mass of colour which served as a groundwork for what he wanted to express... Underpainting in plain red earth (probably Venetian red) for the half-tones, or in white lead. With the same brush dipped in red, black or yellow he worked up the light parts, and in four strokes he could create a remarkably fine figure ... Then he turned the picture to the wall and left it for months without looking at it, until he returned to it and stared critically at it, as if it were a mortal enemy ... By repeated revisions he brought his pictures to a high state of perfection, and while one was drying he worked on another ... He never painted a figure *alla prima*, and used to say that he who improvises can never make a perfect line of poetry. The final touches he softened, occasionally modulating the highest lights

103 TITIAN *Martyrdom of
St Lawrence c.* 1550-5

104 TITIAN *Martyrdom of
St Lawrence* 1564-7

into the half-tones and local colours with his finger; sometimes he
used his finger to dab a dark patch in a corner as an accent, or to
heighten the surface with a bit of red like a drop of blood. He
finished his figures like this and in the last stages he used his fingers
more than his brush.' He died in the middle of a terrible visitation
of the plague, in 1576, having outlived his friends Aretino and
Sansovino, and at the moment when the arts in Venice were divided
between the opulent display of Veronese, and the introspection of
Tintoretto.

Palma Vecchio, born in 1480, and therefore of the same generation as Titian, was, like him, a pupil of Giovanni Bellini, and
equally influenced by Giorgione, though he adds something derived
from Lotto. He can be very Bellinesque in his early altarpieces, but
rapidly adopted Titian's style in later Madonna groups. His spe-

105 TITIAN *Pietà* 1573-6

ciality was the opulent female portrait (*Pl. 106*) – large expanses of
creamy flesh, crimped blonde hair, idealized features, and rich
brocades with a sharp contrast of fine white lawn. But they too
follow Titian's example. He died in 1528. Pordenone, so-called
because he was born in 1483/4 in this small town forty-odd miles
north-west of Venice, was trained outside Venice, and was only
marginally affected by Giorgione. He was fully aware of Central
Italian painting and strongly influenced by Mantegna's illusionism,
and by Sebastiano del Piombo's later mixture of Venetian and

147

106 PALMA VECCHIO
Portrait of a Woman

Michelangelesque forms. He was in Rome about 1516, and Raphael impressed him deeply, so that his style becomes an amalgam of many different inspirations, reacting upon his own passionate and stormy temperament. His *Crucifixion* (*Pl. 107*) in the Cathedral at Cremona of 1521/22, shows an almost German lingering over emotional detail and irrational naturalism, but such works as the organ doors with *Sts Martin and Christopher* in S. Rocco in Venice, of 1528, pose problems about the introduction of Mannerist forms into Venice, for they use some of the commonest Mannerist devices such as large figures in too small a space, strained movement and strong chiaroscuro used for its own sake. He was a highly peripatetic artist whose works are scattered widely over the northwest of Italy, and he was in Venice a good deal from 1527 onwards, during which time he exerted himself to compete with Titian. But the outcome of the contest soon left him with fewer illusions, and changed his admiration for Titian into embittered rivalry, so that he endeavoured to displace him as official painter to the State. He died suddenly in Ferrara in 1539.

148

Lorenzo Lotto presents a very different kind of artist from any of the grand Venetians and their immediate imitators. He was probably born in Venice about 1480, and since his early works are strongly Bellinesque he was probably trained in the Bellini workshop. His first notable work, in a church near Treviso and painted about 1505, is clearly dependent on the type created by Giovanni Bellini in the S. Zaccaria altarpiece, since it has the same disposition of figures and architectural setting. In 1508, still in this strongly Bellinesque style, he painted the large polyptych at Recanati in the Marches (*Pl. 108*), a picture suffused with light, and in particular with light reflected from the vaulting of the loggia which shelters the group of Madonna and Child with attendant saints and angels from the brilliant sun outside. By 1512, in an *Entombment* painted for a confraternity in Jesi, another small Marchigian town, a knowledge of Raphael's *Entombment* seems obvious, crossed perhaps with the dramatic effect of Donatello's Paduan *Lamentations*. During the next ten years he pushed this influence from Central Italian art much further, profiting from Raphael and Fra Bartolommeo, and then in the mid-1520s from Correggio, then from Florentine Mannerists such as Pontormo. His colour too is forced to an incredible brilliance and emotional effect, with violent pinks and reds, cold yellows, and sultry olive greens. There is something German – Altdorfer and Grünewald come quickest to mind – about the colour of his later works, though how he could have seen any of their paintings is a problem: only perhaps in Venice to which he returned frequently between his many provincial commissions, since Venice contained German paintings imported by the northern merchants established there. In some of his very late works his feeling is of a surprising intensity; the 1545 *Pietà* in the Brera has sixteenth-century forms, but the composition makes the picture almost a modernization of one of the late Botticelli *Pietàs*, like the one in the Poldi-Pezzoli in Milan. It is in his portraits, however, that Lotto reaches his highest point (*Pl. 109*). Many of his altarpieces are mannered and unquiet; his portraits consistently show his respect for nature, his innate qualities of design, and a distinguished artistic personality. He always achieves a bold silhouette, an

108 LOTTO *Madonna and Child with Saints* 1508

109 LOTTO *Portrait of Andrea Odoni* 1527

authoritative placing of the sitter on the canvas, and the choice of
a telling gesture, or an evocative still-life. The colour range is
superb: his favourite slaty blues, glowing scarlets, olive greens
and a rich contrast of light and shadow give vivacity and movement
to his portraits, which are as vivid, as masterly, though in an entirely
different way, as any of Titian's. But his great gifts availed him
little; he had a difficult career, struggling with ideas he could follow
but never totally assimilate, and against competition he was ill-
fitted to withstand. He abandoned the effort in 1552 by becoming
a lay brother in the monastery of the Santa Casa at Loreto, and

by 1556 he had died there, so lost and forgotten that no one troubled to record the date of his death. He left a detailed account book, begun in 1538 when he was in Ancona, and from this his later works can be identified; the book also casts much light on the life of a provincial painter in the sixteenth century, as well as providing an insight into Lotto's difficult and rather neurotic personality.

Michiel, in his notes on Giorgione's pictures, remarked that the *Three Philosophers* (*Pl. 87*) had been finished by Sebastiano. This was Sebastiano Luciani later called 'del Piombo', born about 1485, and probably also trained in the Bellini workshop. He was drawn, as Titian was, into the Giorgione circle, as is shown by the small handful of works executed before he removed to Rome permanently in 1511. The core of this group consists of the organ doors of S. Bartolommeo a Rialto of about 1508 (*Pls. 110, 111*), an altarpiece in S. Giovanni Crisostomo (*Pl. 112*), a Madonna, and two or three fancy female heads of indeterminate meaning, but usually exploiting under the guise of a saint the opulent type of beauty currently fashionable in Venice, and the tender and delicate *sfumato* modelling which Giorgione had introduced. The organ doors are painted inside with two life-size figures of Sts Bartholomew and Sebastian within a deep arch against whose darkly shadowed interior they stand silhouetted; the outside of the doors have figures of Sts Louis and Sinibald, each within a deep gold mosaic niche. The colour glows magnificently: St Louis, in a red and gold brocade cope, with a white alb crossed by dark red ribbons, St Sinibald contrasting sombrely in plum and grey, both enveloped in the light which, falling strongly from the left, casts deep shadows into the glowing niches and reflects back on to the figures. In colour, the outside balances the inside, for here the strength of colour is reversed, the St Bartholomew providing the strongest tonal contrast, in his violet cloak lined with green over a dark red robe, to the dazzling nude figure of St Sebastian, his rich flesh tones enhanced by his white loincloth. The figures have a poise and an assurance which has a much more Tuscan quality than one expects in Venice, suggesting the impact of Fra Bartolommeo, who was in Venice in 1508, and the architectural setting, descended from the tradition of Bellini's *sacre conversazioni*, has an unusual – and rather Florentine – largeness and simplicity.

110 SEBASTIANO *St Louis c.* 1508   111 SEBASTIANO *St Sinibald c.* 1508

The altarpiece in S. Giovanni Crisostomo (*Pl. 112*) was painted about 1509; it therefore antedates Bellini's *St Jerome* on the right of the nave which is signed and dated 1513. The comparison is fruitful, for it demonstrates how the old Bellini, then in his seventies, could assimilate the ideas of younger men. Both altarpieces have at the centre an old man reading, oblivious of the saints about him; in fact, the Bellini is in many ways closer to Giorgione's Castel-franco *Madonna* (*Pl. 80*), in that his St Jerome is placed higher and further within the picture space, delimited by a great arch, and the two saints in the foreground seem as detached from him as Giorgione's pair from the enthroned Madonna. Sebastiano's group is tighter knit and more crowded, and the slightly yearning figure of the Baptist on the right looking inwards is balanced by a trio of grandly assured, superb Venetian beauties looking forwards and outwards at the spectator. Again, these are figures in an archi-tectural setting, though one perhaps less well developed than in the organ doors, more accidental and less essentially part of the composition; in this element the Bellini transcends easily. Perhaps, also, the Baptist's pose is too deliberately contrived; in this he contrasts with the majestic female saints who stand like columns come to life below the pedestal of the giant shaft behind the old man immersed in his book.

With Giorgione dead and Titian in Padua, it is difficult to understand why Sebastiano accepted the invitation extended to him by Agostino Chigi, but in 1511 he left Venice to enter, in Rome, first the circle of Raphael and then that of Michelangelo.

112 SEBASTIANO Altarpiece of S. Giovanni Crisostomo *c.* 1509

CHAPTER FOUR

Andrea del Sarto and Correggio

When Leonardo went back to Milan, and Michelangelo went back to Rome to make the Julius Tomb (as he thought), both in 1506, and Raphael left to begin work on the Stanze in 1508, the artistic centre of gravity moved from Florence to Rome. These were to be lean years politically, and until Michelangelo returned to Florence in 1516 to work for the glory of the Medici family imposed as rulers by a Medici Pope, there was little public patronage. Fra Bartolommeo's works were mostly for churches, but he was to die so soon after that his late form of Roman-inspired grandeur found no continuator.

Andrea del Sarto was born in 1486. Vasari says that he was a pupil of Piero di Cosimo, but internal evidence suggests that Raffaellino del Garbo, a late Quattrocento painter with a very fine technique, may have been, if not his formal teacher, certainly his most important one. By about 1506 he was sharing a studio with Franciabigio, who had been a pupil of Fra Bartolommeo's assistant Albertinelli, and in 1511 they were joined by the sculptor Jacopo Sansovino on his return from Rome. About this time, Sarto had Pontormo and Rosso as pupils, and late in 1524 Vasari, then thirteen, came to him as a pupil for about two years. Vasari's short connection gives great verisimilitude to his life of Andrea del Sarto. It is obvious that he loathed Lucrezia, his master's wife, and that he did not have a very high opinion of Sarto's character, so that it is difficult to estimate how much of his interpretation is plain libel, and how much of it is based on an all too intimate knowledge.

Sarto's first works were frescoes of the *Miracles of S. Filippo Benizzi (Pl. 113)* in the entrance courtyard of the SS. Annunziata, painted in 1509/10, followed in 1511 by his first frescoes in the

113 SARTO *The Miracles of S. Filippo Benizzi* 1509-10

little cloister of the lay confraternity of the Scalzo. This commission for monochrome frescoes of the life of the Baptist (*Pl. 114*) continued intermittently until 1526. In 1513/14 he was again working in the Annunziata courtyard, painting the superb fresco of the *Birth of the Virgin* (*Pl. 115*), which contains in the group of women in attendance upon the new mother a portrait of the beautiful Lucrezia, who was widowed in 1516, and whom he married shortly after. In the early summer of 1518 he accepted an invitation from Francis I to go to Fontainebleau, but only one or two paintings can be associated with this visit, which ended late in 1519, when he came home again ostensibly to fetch his wife. Vasari's story is that Sarto embezzled a large sum of money given him by Francis I to buy works of art, and he certainly made a very large bank deposit immediately upon his return and later built himself a house and studio. He probably visited Rome soon after the French journey, lived through the terrible siege of Florence in 1529/30, and died of plague immediately afterwards. Vasari's unflattering account of Lucrezia not only accuses her of ruining her husband's career, but also of abandoning him on his deathbed.

156

114 SARTO *St John the Baptist preaching* 1515

Sarto's great gifts are such that he has been acclaimed as the perfect artist, the painter who never made a mistake. His impeccable draughtsmanship is full of feeling, his simple colour schemes are tender, his dazzling technique, whether in oil or fresco, makes difficulties seem non-existent. The influence of Leonardo led him to develop soft modelling and the telltale smile, and later he combined these with an unmistakable type of face with dark smudgy eyes, short nose, and wide slightly open mouth – Lucrezia's famous face. The really great development is in his use of chiaroscuro. If one compares his most outstanding altarpiece, the *Madonna of the Harpies* (*Pl. 139*) – so called from the little figures on the pedestal – of 1517, with any of the grand Raphael ones (the *Sistine Madonna* (*Pl. 67*) is almost contemporary) the first thing that is clear is the derivation from Raphael. The Madonna has close links with such Raphaels as the roundel of *Poetry* (*Pl. 41*) in the Segnatura ceiling, and there is the same exaltation of the Mother of God to a superhuman state, the same stress on the God Child,

115 SARTO *Birth of the Virgin* 1514

the same subtlety in the alternation of the poses of the two saints and in their relationship to the Madonna and to the spectator, the same spatial affinity. In the Raphael the field is closed by the empty sky and by the sharp frontal plane of the curtain and the little angels; in the Sarto there is a wall behind the Madonna and the shallow space is marked off in front by the step on which the small pedestal stands. There is a similar idealization in the Madonna and the saints, the same restriction to the barest essentials of a *sacra conversazione*. But when one considers the way in which this simple group is constructed in terms of chiaroscuro, then the differences become vital to an understanding of the new trends which Sarto represents in Florence. The light in the Raphael is an even, clear illumination which makes the subject plain; the Sarto has a glancing, moving, intermittent light which gives mystery and emotion to the group. It is composed of fitful gleams, which strike and glance away again, so that the picture becomes a vision, half-glimpsed in a half-light, and the patches of light and dark are as episodic as passing sunlight.

This treatment of light is consistent throughout the artist's *œuvre*, for it is present in a tentative form as early as the Dresden *Marriage of St Catherine* of about 1512, and is at its grandest in the late *Madonna and Saints* (*Pl. 116*) in the Pitti painted in 1525/6. The use of this kind of patchwork of light and shadow is less pronounced in his frescoes, largely because the medium lends itself less readily to strong chiaroscuro (the difference of technique often vitiates comparisons between frescoes and easel pictures); yet it occurs. The magnificent *Birth of the Virgin* (*Pl. 115*) of 1514 combines a shadowy background with sharply stressed figures and objects, like the sheet, the towel on the woman's lap, the bunched up bed-curtains; the Scalzo frescoes, which are his longest series, use this device constantly. In fact, the Scalzo frescoes may have encouraged this kind of lighting by being in monochrome, thus

116 SARTO *Madonna and Child with Saints c.* 1525-6

tending to exaggerate contrasts of light, and because of the variation in the normal fresco technique which he used for them – a very thick, impasted fresco laid upon a middle tint. Though Michelangelo was working in Florence throughout the greater part of Sarto's later career, only rarely is there a reflection of his influence – Isaac, in the late *Sacrifice of Abraham* (*Pl. 118*), in its dependence on the figure of Victory (*Pl. 117*) is one instance – though he is constantly affected by the power and vigour of Michelangelo's drawing. What is more striking is the use of Dürer's engravings. Vasari is very hard upon Pontormo for doing this, but he passes over Sarto's borrowings from them in silence.

Franciabigio, with whom Sarto shared a studio for a couple of years, was born in 1482/3 and died in 1525. He was a channel through which the influence of Fra Bartolommeo reached Sarto, since Franciabigio was Albertinelli's pupil until the latter abandoned his partnership with the Frate to become an innkeeper in 1511, at the same moment that Sarto finally found that he could tolerate Piero di Cosimo's eccentricities no longer. At first their styles were very close, but by 1514, when both artists completed frescoes in the Annunziata courtyard, painted virtually in competition, it

160

118 SARTO *Sacrifice of Abraham*

was clear that Andrea had excelled him, for in a rage Franciabigio destroyed part of his *Marriage of the Virgin*. His *Last Supper* in the Convent of the Calza, also of 1514, is Ghirlandaio's old fashioned scheme brought up to date by vaguely Leonardesque gestures and groupings, and by a striving towards Raphael's ideal classicism of type. He is at his best as a portrait painter, with something of Lotto's introspective sensitiveness (*Pl. 119*).

At first sight, one would not think of connecting the hard, linear, exploratory style of Mantegna with Correggio's soft modelling, fluidity of pose and melting tenderness of expression. Yet there is a tradition that he was Mantegna's pupil. He was born, probably in 1489, at Correggio, some thirty miles from Parma, and he could have been in Mantegna's workshop in Mantua, also some thirty miles distant, at about fifteen years of age, and a pupil for at least two years before Mantegna died in September 1506. The point at which tradition gives way to evidence is in the resemblances between Correggio's earliest works and Mantegna's late ones. The *Madonna of St Francis* (*Pl. 120*), so-called from the St Francis in the group of four saints at the base of the throne, is his earliest certain work, and was commissioned in 1514. The pose of the Madonna and the gesture of her right hand is so close to Mantegna's late *Madonna of Victory* (*Pl. 121*) that it is patent that one inspired the other. Correggio also adapted the trellis of the arbour behind Mantegna's Madonna for the framework of his first big decoration. Moreover, if one moves outside the certain works, some small devotional pictures attributed to Correggio point firmly to his having come from Mantegna's circle. The influence of Leonardo is obvious in the *Madonna of St Francis* – in the Baptist, for instance – but by this date this was a commonplace throughout northern and central Italy. Correggio seems also to have gone further afield than Mantua, probably to Florence, for there are aspects of his tender handling, and the sweetness of his Madonna and Child groups, and in the way the light and shadow form islands of brilliance and depth rather than a flowing illumination, that suggest a powerful influence from Andrea del Sarto. His life is fairly well documented, but there are quite long gaps when he could have been away from home: from 1511 to 1514, from mid-1515 to late

1516, for most of 1518 (when he was probably in Parma), and again a long gap of nearly two years in 1531/32. He uses the grand poses and gestures developed by Roman and Florentine artists, and a similar articulation of his pictures by swinging rhythms; in his later works, also, there is an intensity of religious emotion, and complexity in the formal composition, that presage the movement and drama of the Baroque.

The first of his decorations is in the Camera di S. Paolo in Parma, probably painted in 1518 (*Pl. 122*). It is a vaulted room, the ceiling of which is covered by frescoes representing a trellised arbour (like Mantegna's in the *Madonna of Victory*, and also recalling the divisions in the Farnesina decoration) with lunettes below filled with allegorical subjects in grisaille. It raises immediately the question of where he had been before this, for it is difficult to conceive of any artist not aware of the decoration of the Sistine Ceiling or the Farnesina creating *putti* of this heroic kind and mythologies

119 FRANCIABIGIO *Portrait of a Man* 1514

120 CORREGGIO *Madonna of St Francis*
c. 1514-15

121 MANTEGNA *Madonna of Victory*

122 CORREGGIO Camera di S. Paolo, Parma (detail) *c.* 1518

of this lighthearted character. The problem is made more acute
by the dome of S. Giovanni Evangelista in Parma, painted between
1520 and 1524, on the theme of St John's visions on Patmos
(*Pls. 123, 127*). Here he is clearly inspired by Mantegna, with a ring
of apostles seated round the cornice below the clouds through which
floats upwards the figure of the Risen Christ. The strongly
illusionist figures in sharp foreshortening, the ascending Christ
soaring upwards into the cloudy sky, go back ultimately to the
ceiling of the Camera degli Sposi, which did not have a great deal of
influence until Correggio and Giulio Romano, since it was in the
private apartments of the Gonzaga family, and therefore not easily
to be seen. On the other hand, several of the figures in the ceiling
are clearly dependent on Michelangelo's Sistine Ceiling, and there
is an additional fragment of evidence in his practice of using his
cartoons twice over, the second time with the figures reversed.

165

123 CORREGGIO Dome of S. Giovanni Evangelista, Parma 1520-3

124 CORREGGIO *Madonna of St Jerome 'Il Giorno' c.* 1527-8

125 CORREGGIO *Nativity 'La Notte' c.* 1530

He does this for some major figures and even more frequently in the angels and the *putti*; Michelangelo also did it in the *Ignudi* in the earliest stages of the Ceiling (*Pls. 61, 62*) and throughout for the *putti* behind the thrones, and the spandrel figures on either side of them. It is an old device, but one which it is surprising to find revived in such a context and on such a scale, though Parmigianino was to use it later at the Steccata.

The third great dome decoration is in the cathedral in Parma, and was done between 1526 and 1530 (*Pl. 126*). This is a much larger dome than S. Giovanni, more pointed, octagonal, and on squinches instead of pendentives. The angles have been plastered out in the upper part so as to make a rounded surface, and the shape of the squinches forced Correggio to strengthen the chiaroscuro in the figures he painted on them. The decoration (which represents the Assumption) is arranged in rising tiers: the apostles stand upon the cornice at the base, between the round windows that light the dome, and above them rise, like so many concentric wreaths, a mass of moving figures, twisting, turning, breaking in and out of the clouds, supporting the rising figure of the Virgin as she soars heavenwards. All the devices he had used in the Camera and S. Giovanni are also used here; there is good reason for believing that Correggio drew from small models which he posed for the figures of the angels, for instance, and he also used the reversed cartoon method for variety in poses. Both Correggio's domes are strangely closer to Baroque than they are to other Renaissance works; the congested, swirling mass of figures, the ecstatic quality of the gestures and expressions, the way in which the light suffuses the groups, seem to leap ahead by at least a century. The same feeling pervades his many altarpieces and mythological pictures. Only once, after the early *Madonna of St Francis* (*Pl. 120*), did he follow the High Renaissance form of raising the Madonna well above her votaries; in general he does just the opposite, and makes her the centre of a confused crowd of adoring saints and angels, pressing in upon her from all around, so that she draws the eye into the depth of the picture along the gestures and movements of the surrounding figures. He uses, too, the delicate *sfumato* technique of Leonardo, with limpid colour and without the murky shadows of Leonardo, or the dark, shot, effects of Giulio Romano

126 CORREGGIO Dome of Parma Cathedral 1526-30

or the Florentine Mannerists. In the famous nightpiece of the *Nativity* (*Pl. 125*) the Child lying in His mother's arms in the manger is the source of light for the whole picture: Virgin, shepherds, angels in the very solid clouds overhead are suffused with the light emanating physically from the Infant, underlining in the most deliberate way the literal significance of the texts concerning the Light born amid darkness that comprehended it not. The Child had often been portrayed emitting rays of light, but it is rare (though it does occur in the Netherlands with Geergten) that the Child is made the only source of light, but for the pallid dawn suffusing the distant sky. In this picture, Correggio stands at the head of a

169

128 CORREGGIO *Danäe* c. 1531-2

7 CORREGGIO Dome of S. Giovanni
vangelista (detail of pl. 123)

long line of Tenebrists, for this treatment of the scene becomes common enough in the seventeenth century.

The almost equally famous *Madonna with St Jerome (Pl. 124)* is the absolute antithesis (hence the contrasting nicknames of 'Night' and 'Day' which the pictures acquired in the eighteenth century), for here all the figures are suffused with light, which weaves in and out, and across the forms, so that the picture has a restless, flickering quality. The composition is a favourite form of his: a short, shallow pyramid, tipped backwards with huge repoussoir figures on either side, and the front plane stressed by some *putti*. He frequently gives this shape to his groups, in his dome pendentives as well as in his easel pictures, in mythologies as well as religious subjects. For instance, in the *Danäe (Pl. 128)*, of about 1531/32, the small *putti* serve to push back into space the soft, sensual body of Danäe, who trails her slender, golden leg over the edge of the bed as she leans backwards on the pillows, and the same device is found in the *Jupiter and Antiope* of about 1523/24. These are the secular counterparts of his tender, ecstatic Madonnas and saints: meltingly sensual eroticism is inherent in both. He learned early the haunting quality of the Leonardo half-smile, for it flickers constantly over the faces of his figures, saints, Venuses, Madonnas, and nymphs alike, and his gifts as a colourist were such that Giulio Romano, faced with the *Danäe* and the *Leda*, newly arrived in his patron's collection in Mantua, declared them to be of such perfection that he had never seen colouring anywhere that could compare.

CHAPTER FIVE

Michelangelo in Florence

The first project upon which Pope Leo X proposed to employ
Michelangelo was a façade for Brunelleschi's church of S. Lorenzo
– the Medici family church, a stone's throw from the Medici palace
in Florence. He began work in 1516; a contract was signed in 1518
for the façade, which was to be executed in eight years (this meant
that it had to be worked on simultaneously with the Tomb, the
marbles for which he ordered to be sent to Florence). The design
called for an architectural frame to be filled with sculpture – 'in
architecture and sculpture the cynosure of all Italy' as Michelangelo
himself described it, and in fact from all accounts it is clear that
it was to be a combination of the Julius Tomb and the Sistine
Ceiling. Shortly after signing the contract, he was told that the
marble was not to be bought from Carrara, but extracted from a
new quarry at Pietrasanta in Florentine territory. To get the marble
out a road had to be built; then the Carrarese, fearful lest their
major export should be thus frustrated, organized a strike among
the bargemen to prevent Pietrasanta stone from being shipped up
the Arno to Florence; then Michelangelo's enemies in Rome
persuaded one of the signatories to the 1516 Tomb contract to
demand performance; finally, after further wrangles, mostly over
money, the contract for the façade was abruptly annulled. Three
years had passed.

More or less as a consolation for the disaster over the façade,
Leo X then thought of the idea of commissioning, not just a tomb,
but a funerary chapel for the family, to be built inside the empty
and partially built shell of the walls of another sacristy in S. Lorenzo, a counterpart to Brunelleschi's Old Sacristy. In order to
'help' the sculptor, but possibly also with the idea of containing
his enthusiasm within the limits of the possible, an architect was

129 MICHELANGELO
Madonna and Child 1524-7

assigned to him for work on the structure, but Michelangelo soon disposed of him. The first plans for the Medici tombs – there were to be four of them – took the form of a free-standing edifice so ominously reminiscent of the Julius Tomb that Cardinal Giulio de' Medici would have none of it, and finally a series of wall-tombs was decided upon, to be erected within an architectural framework designed by Michelangelo himself.

The New Sacristy (*Pl. 130*), as it is called, is a small centrally planned building, much higher than Brunelleschi's Old Sacristy, but vaguely like it in that it has a small domed choir at one end, and a system of *pietra serena* pilasters and entablature, and pedimented windows, and is surmounted by a hemi-spherical dome, though this one is coffered *all'antica*. Michelangelo began by so arranging the internal architecture that the doorway into the chapel from the church was placed obliquely, so that the inner part with the door did not come right in the corner of the chapel, as it does in the Old Sacristy, but matched the position of the small doors leading into the little vestries on either side of the choir. He then devised five more doors, so that there are two in each wall in a perfectly symmetrical arrangement. When all the doors are

130 MICHELANGELO Medici Chapel (interior)

closed the chapel becomes a sealed world, inhabited only by the dead and by the priest at the altar. He placed the altar, not as it was in the Old Sacristy, well within the small choir, but on the outer edge of it, so that the celebrant faced into the chapel. Since this meant that there was no place for an altarpiece, he designed the wall facing the altar to contain a group of the *Madonna and Child* (*Pl. 129*), flanked by *Sts Cosmas and Damian*, the Medici patron saints; this provided an altarpiece across the width of the chapel, and also a focal point. Furthermore, the final design of the two tombs (*Pls. 131, 132*) on the side walls contained figures symbolical of the dead men, who look towards the Madonna group on the

131 MICHELANGELO Tomb of Lorenzo de' Medici

end wall: thus, at the memorial mass for the family, the priest's congregation is the dead, who turn towards the intercessory Madonna, while the patron saints plead their cause.

There are many drawings for Michelangelo's projects for the tombs: the final form seems to have been one on each side wall, and a double one facing the altar, but of this project only the two side tombs were erected, and they were never finished. The dead men so commemorated were, in fact, not particularly important members of the family – Giuliano, Duke of Nemours and son of Lorenzo the Magnificent, and his nephew Lorenzo, Duke of Urbino: it was to this Lorenzo that Leo X gave the duchy of Urbino

132 MICHELANGELO Tomb of Giuliano de' Medici

133 MICHELANGELO *Night*

135 MICHELANGELO *Dusk*

134 MICHELANGELO *Day*

136 MICHELANGELO *Dawn*

when he took it from Julius II's heir, Michelangelo's much tried patron for the Julius Tomb, and it is one of the ironies of the situation that Michelangelo's work in the Medici Chapel was in many ways a substitute for the first Tomb, and like it also remained unfinished.

In deep niches over the sarcophagi are figures emblematic of the dead men, each conceived, not as a portrait but as an ideal representation of a state of mind – Giuliano as the Active Life, and Lorenzo as the Contemplative Life. On the lid of each sarcophagus are figures representing the Times of Day – the positive times of Night and Day for the Active Life; the more indecisive times of Dawn and Dusk for the Contemplative Life. Both men are clad in classical armour, Giuliano in an alert pose of arrested movement, Lorenzo relaxed and thoughtful, head resting on his hand and face shadowed by the raised visor of his helmet. The Times of Day are massive, heavy figures, so large that they appear to be slipping off the lid of the sarcophagus which they overhang. *Night (Pl. 133)* with shadowed face and Athena's owl beneath her knee, leaning upon the grotesque mask of the unreality of dreams, poppies at her feet, a star and crescent moon crowning her bowed and sleeping head; *Day (Pl. 134)* is full of vigour and energy, glowering over his shoulder in a pose so uncomfortable that it underlines the transitoriness of his position; *Dawn (Pl. 136)* lifts herself from her uneasy sleep, half awake only, dragged unwillingly into consciousness, heavy limbed and lethargic; *Dusk (Pl. 135)* seems to be sinking into an old man's hazy dream, troubled and withdrawn. All the figures have expressions of grief and movements of unwilling action as if, to use Michelangelo's own idea, they had in truth been locked within the stone and he, by freeing them, had done them an injury by dragging them into a world of sorrow. They were to have been completed by four figures of River Gods, one below each sarcophagus figure, to personify the four Rivers of Hades, which Dante had equated with the tears of humanity. The *Madonna and Child (Pl. 129)*, towards whom the dead men turn, is a compact group, the Madonna leaning slightly forward as if to shelter the Child twisted round on her lap, burying His head against her and shielding His face with His arm, as if He were trying to escape from the sight of death and the transitoriness of earthly things. The patron saints are stalwart old men, like classical philosophers, but with troubled faces and expressions almost of foreboding. The imagery of the whole chapel, silent and enclosed, expresses, in a blend of Christian and Platonic thought, the idea of the House of the Dead, where the soul, freed from the travails of the world and returned to its state of pure immortality, in the realization of the uncertainty of human life and fortune, and in the contemplation of the eternal and the Divine, awaits the Resurrection.

The figures of the two dukes and the patron saints were brought to a high state of finish. Of the remaining figures none is complete, parts being barely freed from the block, other parts finished – like the *Night* – to a high polish. Michelangelo worked on them all together, and used his assistants for preparatory work, for finishing under his direction, and for the architecture. This is very complicated, for the various niches and the tabernacles over the doors create a mass of different planes within the structure, so that it is difficult to work out the relationship of the parts to each other. This complexity was deliberate, and fits in with the puzzling function of the doors, the difference in size between the dukes and the sarcophagus figures below them, and the curiously uncertain effect created by the huge figures balanced precariously upon the lids of the tombs. One thing is very clear: though the various elements are inspired by classical architectural forms, in detail and in their combination they are completely original. Michelangelo is not re-using the forms of the past so much as creating new ones: the *stipiti* – those narrow pilasters on either side of the niches in the tabernacles over the doors that become wider as they rise – the forms of the capitals, of the pediments jammed tightly between the pilasters of the *pietra serena* articulation, the swags in the frieze, the consoles supporting the pediments and the tabernacles, all these are classical ideas, but here they are given totally new forms and functions.

When Lorenzo de' Medici left his famous library to the city, it was decided to house it in the monastery of S. Lorenzo, adjoining the family parish church. The project for the Library became, therefore, like the family sepulchral chapel, part of the S. Lorenzo complex which started with the abortive project for the façade.

137 MICHELANGELO Laurenziana Library. Vestibule wall 1524-6

Michelangelo's first projects for the Library were on such a scale that they would have involved almost total reconstruction of the convent and the adjoining square. In 1524 more modest provision was eventually made, on Clement VII's instructions, by building a further storey over the top of the refectory and by making the access to it through a vestibule at one end (*Pl. 138*), adjoining the church and giving on to the cloister. The Pope also rejected Michelangelo's first project for the top-lighting of this vestibule, and insisted that it should have normal windows: this meant that he was forced to make it very much higher in order to accommodate the windows in a top storey, so as to retain the architectural system he had devised for the inside walls of the vestibule. The central part of the room is taken up by a huge flight of steps, free-standing like a piece of sculpture, with three flights separated by balustrades uniting into one flight immediately before the door, the steps of the central flight curved so that they appear to be flowing like molten stone down from the library and spreading across the floor. In fact, Michelangelo did not build these steps, for they were made by Vasari and Amannati and based freely on Michelangelo's sketchy projects sent from Rome in the 1550s. The walls of the vestibule present several odd features (*Pl. 137*): they are divided into three bays each by pairs of columns engaged in the walls and supporting an entablature which breaks back over them, not forward as might be expected; between these pairs of columns are panels which project well in front of the columns, and these carry large tabernacle windows with fluted *stipiti* at the sides and pediments above, triangular in the centre and segmental at the sides. Above the windows are shallow, curved niches surmounted by small lintels and surrounded by decorative beading; below the columns, and the string course on which they stand, are heavy consoles which appear to be bearing the weight of the order set into the wall. On the outside of the building, the system is reversed, with heavily pedimented blind windows inset between strip buttresses, though this part of the work is a twentieth-century completion. Actually, the arrangement of the walls inside is not nearly so wayward as it at first seems, for the columns and consoles set into the wall are part of the piers which bear the weight of the building, while the projecting panels bearing the windows are really infilling between these structural members. The effect of the arrangement is of an exterior façade turned inwards. The Library inside continues the system with the great book-rests of the bays projecting inwards where the piers and buttresses strengthen the wall between the panels bearing the windows. The doors, too, present unusual features in that they have multiple frames and pediments, set tightly one within another, so that the system of planes is complex and difficult to work out. It is in connection with the Laurenziana that Vasari comments on Michelangelo's inventiveness, and his insistence that he never imitated· the antique, but was creating new forms on a par with antiquity.

Despite Michelangelo's initial enthusiasm the progress of all the S. Lorenzo works was beset by troubles. Lawsuits were threatened by the Julius heirs; there were money troubles because Cardinal Giulio, when he eventually became Pope in 1523, faced grave political difficulties; also the Pope kept pressing other commissions on the artist (the commission for the Laurenziana Library was, in fact, given in 1524), and was fertile in new and grandiose ideas rather than helpful over providing for the completion of those already started. Michelangelo agreed to accept the commission for the Chapel in 1520; the structure was ready and the tombs themselves begun in 1524, but nothing was finished when work stopped in April, 1527. In May came the Sack of Rome, followed in Florence by a republican rising, the expulsion of the Medici, and the setting up of a new Republic. In 1528, despite the Pope's pleas that he should continue working for him, Michelangelo began working on the fortifications of the city, and later became a member of the council for its defence. He fled in 1529 suspecting – rightly as it turned out – that Florence would be betrayed to the besieging armies of the reconciled Pope and Emperor, but returned to help defend it, and after its fall he was received back into papal favour on condition that he went on with the Chapel. He was now in his middle fifties; partly because of the trials he had undergone with the Tomb, and with the rigours of Pope Julius's patronage, partly because of the tragedy of recent events in Florence, partly because of his natural pessimism, the heart had gone out of him, and he wanted nothing more than to have done with Florence and the Medici and to return to Rome. Many years later, when the unfinished Chapel was finally opened to the public, an admirer addressed a poem to him, extolling the rendering of sleep in the *Night* as so lifelike that if one spoke to her she would reply; he answered with a quatrain of tragic bitterness: 'Sweet to me is sleep, and even more to be like stone While wrong and shame endure; Not to see, nor to feel, is my good fortune. Therefore, do not wake me; speak softly here.'

Work on the Library stopped in 1526, before the work on the Chapel. Together these two works, and the designs for the façade constitute Michelangelo's first essays in architecture. They are the prelude to his later career in Rome, and an extension of the architectural aspects of the Julius Tomb and the Sistine Ceiling.

In 1534 he returned to Florence from a visit to Rome to attend the deathbed of his father. He then felt that there was nothing now to keep him there, for there was no prospect of finishing any of the S. Lorenzo works. He left the city in September 1534 to settle in Rome, where he remained for the rest of his long life. Two days after he arrived Pope Clement VII died: his next patron was the new Pope, the Farnese Paul III.

139 SARTO *Madonna of the Harpies* 1517

The story of the High Renaissance contains several moments when it is possible to take stock of what has already happened, and examine the way later developments stem from, or are influenced by, what has gone before. One such climacteric came in 1520. In that year Raphael died at the height of his career and at a moment when his art was poised to take a new direction, and Michelangelo began the planning of the Medici Chapel, to evolve for it a style which would lead him to completely different modes of expression from those he had used in the Sistine Ceiling. Another was in 1527, the year when the Sack of Rome filled all Christendom with a shock of horror and shame and unrighteous exultation, even greater than the shock caused by the fall of Constantinople in 1453. There was yet a third in the middle 1530s. Andrea del Sarto's death in 1531 removed prematurely the one considerable Florentine who pursued, with almost unchanging directness, ideals that can be defined as essentially High Renaissance ones: clarity, sensitivity, simplicity and nobility of form, allied to richness of colour, a magnificent and poetic use of light and shadow, sheer physical beauty, and technical brilliance. Correggio's early death in 1534 eliminated an artist whose style, though more ecstatic, more emotional, than Sarto's, expressed very similar ideas. In 1534 Michelangelo left Florence for good, thereby relegating it – and this despite the real achievements of the next generation – to a subsidiary position, so great was not only his genius but also the aura of his fame. Michelangelo's very long life (he lived to be eighty-eight) meant that the span of his creative years, lasting until 1564, gave him a career three times as long as Raphael's, and twice as long as any of his major contemporaries except Titian. In fact, Michelangelo outlived several of the younger men upon whom his own later Roman style was a decisive formative influence.

It seems reasonable, therefore, to consider the years from about 1495 to about 1535 as a unit, though even this brief period presents several facets. One of the most interesting of these reflects the opinions which were held at the time concerning the differences of style between works done in the years immediately after the turn of the century and those of the 1520s and 1530s. The distinction between the early years – Bramante's Roman years and the beginning of Raphael's Roman career – and the later Roman works of Raphael can almost always be defined as a question of enrichment. The early years, now extolled as the highest point of clarity and balance, were then considered only as a preparatory stage leading to the rich ornamentation and complexity of the last decade of his short life. Those characteristics of order and control, which were so powerful a reaction against the chaotic elaboration of much of late Quattrocento art, and for which one could quite appropriately borrow Winckelmann's description of Greek art as 'calm grandeur and noble simplicity', were held at the time to have produced no more than dryness and a chilly bareness. It was the later Cinquecento wealth of decorative enrichment, complicated planning, elaborate poses, graceful gestures, and dramatic facial expressions, that were considered both as the true reflection of the antique and representative of the new style. And this is exact, in that the two most recent important discoveries of antique sculpture were the Apollo Belvedere and the Laocoon – one the epitome of grace and refinement, the other highly dramatic, emotional, complicated in its poses and its use of three figures linked physically and psychologically to form a narrative group. In considering the impact of classical Rome upon Renaissance art, it must never be forgotten that the antique itself changed through new and exciting discoveries, and new ways of looking at and interpreting the past, so that the classical influences which helped to form the Early Renaissance and those which worked so powerfully upon the High Renaissance are the same in name, but often very different indeed in nature. The differences between the House of Raphael (*Pl. 74*), for instance, and the Palazzo Branconio dell'Aquila are not only the measure of a change in architectural thought between Bramante and Raphael, but are also indicative of a change in the kind of classicism fashionable, admired, and imitated a decade later. Vasari is explicit about

140 TITIAN *Diana and Actaeon* 1559

the importance attached to decoration in the Preface to the third
part of his Lives: 'This spontaneity enables the artist to enhance
his work by adding innumerable inventive details, and, as it were, a
pervasive beauty to what is merely artistically correct. ...abundance
of beautiful clothes, the imaginative details, charming colours,
many kinds of building and various landscapes in depth that we
see depicted today'.

Venice was the only part of Italy to escape the worst ravages
of the long wars that culminated in the Sack of Rome and the Siege

141 TITIAN *Tarquin and Lucretia* c. 1571

142 TITIAN *Jacopo Strada* 1568

of Florence. It was also the part that remained least profoundly affected by the changes in religious thought stemming from the Counter-Reformation and the Council of Trent. In Venice, therefore, the High Renaissance seems to linger on with the kind of magnificent afterglow that a long and brilliant sunset imparts to a summer's day at a moment when the weather is about to break. It is true that the later years of Titian and the architecture of Sansovino appear as a mature and thoughtful extension of the confident splendours of the early years of the century. But Sansovino was a refugee from the disasters that tore the political, artistic and religious fabric of Italy apart, and all his architecture was created after the Sack, so that his style is better seen in the context of later ideas and forms. The same argument applies also to Sanmicheli.

Titian's life was as long as Michelangelo's, beginning and ending a decade later. There are, in his art, breaks as distinct as those in Michelangelo's, though they are expressed in a different way. As a painter exclusively, he was one artist, so to speak, whose style changed, modified, developed, through one art over almost seventy years, where Michelangelo was three artists, whose ideas were expressed in sculpture, painting and architecture, and whose ideas in one art were constantly modified by his experiences in another medium. The Medici Chapel contains ideas which are new – startlingly so – but it is also in many ways a continuation of processes of thought which start quite clearly in the Sistine Ceiling, and both the Ceiling and the Chapel are expressions of ideas which Michelangelo first conceived for the Julius Tomb. The architecture of the Laurenziana is perhaps the moment when a major change of thought occurred, yet not only is it contemporary with the Chapel, but some of the forms he used in it are extensions of ideas first put forward in the Chapel, and in turn these works conditioned his approach to the *Last Judgement*, the Farnese Palace, St Peter's, and the Campidoglio. The changes in Titian's art are both stylistic and conceptual: as he grew older his technique changed from the limpid clarity, the warm sunniness of, say, *Sacred and Profane Love* (*Pl. 89*) or the *Andrians* to the more clotted richness of the later *poesie* – the *Diana and Actaeon* (*Pl. 140*) or the *Lucretia* (*Pl. 141*). The same technical changes appear, naturally, in his religious pictures as well: the calm, triumphant serenity of the *Pesaro Ma*-

donna (*Pl. 95*) is succeeded by the greater emotion, expressiveness in colour, design and dramatic feeling of the late Prado *Entombments*. What also changes is the kind of subject that inspired him, or the manner of his approach to it. Instead of the joyous openness of, say, the *Bacchus and Ariadne* (*Pl. 92*) where, despite the dark undertones of the myth, all is light and colour and revelry, he later choses the story of Actaeon, or the unhappy Callisto, or the betrayed Lucretia – dark horrors concealed beneath the brilliant colour and the surface richness. In his religious works, the delight and innocence of the early Madonna pictures – the National Gallery *Madonna and Child with St Catherine*, or the Louvre *Madonna with the Rabbit*, for example – give way to darker, more heroic subjects such as the horrific *Martyrdom of St Lawrence* (*Pls. 103, 104*) or the tragic *Crowning with Thorns*, full of flames and torchlight, agony and terror, blood and violence. It is not just a matter of age and maturity bringing with them pessimism and an acceptance of suffering, since there are enough examples of great artists who lived to be old men – Tiepolo, Ingres, or Renoir for instance – whose work never expresses a sense of doom. In Titian, the reflection of the changed climate of the mid-century affects his selection of motives rather than his vision, in that he does not see his subjects in terms of fantastic light effects or strange perspective arranged for its dramatic possibilities, as Veronese and Tintoretto later do, but only uses them incidentally as they fit the chosen subject, like subordinate clauses used to help the meaning he wishes to convey. The distinction may be a subtle one, but there is a difference of character between Titian and his great successors. Even in his portraits, usually the last form to be affected by such stylistic changes, this difference also appears, as may immediately be seen by comparing the late *Jacopo Strada* (*Pl. 142*) with the early *Young Man with a Glove* (*Pl. 98*), or the confident serene patricians in the *Pesaro Madonna* (*Pl. 95*) with the more troubled faces and expressions in the great Vendramin family portrait. Yet, for all these subtle transitions of mood and thought, Titian's art retains a splendid homogeneity and, even at his most questing moments, he retains his poise and a kind of forthright confidence. Fear and doubt never seem to have touched him as they touched Michelangelo, and he never knew physical danger as Rosso and Parmigianino knew it; his darker subjects seem to suggest more a spiritual catharsis than the vivid experiences which lie behind the tormented imagination of many of the Mannerists.

If one looks from the eager, confident serenity of the *School of Athens* (*Pl. 39*) or the *David* (*Pl. 25*), to the complexity and anxiety running as an undercurrent in the *Transfiguration* (*Pl. 77*) or the Medici Chapel, then the change of mood, perception, thought, and environment, marks the end of an era and the opening of a new stage. Just as the mid-1490s were a watershed between the Early and the High Renaissance, so the mid-1530s form a watershed between the High Renaissance and the art of the second half of the sixteenth century in which Mannerism is so conspicuous and compelling a feature. Moreover, although a trickle of Italian ideas and forms spread north of the Alps in the first years of the century, it was not until the second half that the trickle became a flood and the whole of Western Europe was affected by, and came eventually to participate in, the Renaissance.

Selected Bibliography

This is a brief list of the major books, mostly in English. All periodical literature has been excluded, and only a selection of monographs on major artists has been given.

Sources

By far the most important source for the period is VASARI's *Vite* (1550 and, much enlarged, 1568). There is a full translation in 10 volumes by G. du C. de Vere, London, 1912-15. The best English version of the most important *Lives* is by George Bull, Penguin Classics, London, 1965. The standard Italian edition is that by G. Milanesi, Florence, 9 volumes, 1878-85, but there is an excellent modern edition, published by the Club del Libro, Milan, 7 volumes (in progress), 1962-. A national edition is in preparation; so far only one volume (Florence, 1966) has appeared.

A selection of translated sources will be found in E. HOLT, *A Documentary History of Art*, Vol. II, New York, 1958, and R. KLEIN and H. ZERNER, *Italian Art 1500-1600*, New Jersey, 1966. A. BLUNT's *Artistic Theory in Italy, 1450-1600*, Oxford, 1940, deals critically with these and other sources. The standard bibliography is the indispensable *Letteratura Artistica* by J. VON SCHLOSSER-MAGNINO, ed. O. Kurz, Florence, 1956. Most of the sixteenth-century writers have been republished recently in the *Scrittori d'Italia* series.

Historical background

P. BURKE, *The Renaissance*, London, 1964
D. HAY, *The Italian Renaissance*, Cambridge, 1961
P. LAVEN, *Renaissance Italy, 1464-1534*, London, 1966
New Cambridge Modern History, Vols. I and II, 1957 and 1962

General histories

A. CHASTEL, *The Age of Humanism, 1480-1530*, London, 1963
H. WÖLFFLIN, *Classic Art* (trans.) London, 1952

Architecture

P. MURRAY, *Architecture of the Italian Renaissance*, London, 1963
(paperback ed., New York, 1966)
P. LETAROUILLY, Edifices de Rome moderne, 4 vols., Paris, 1840-57
and 6 vols., London, 1928-30 (excellent illustrations)
STEGMANN-GEYMULLER, *Architecture of the Renaissance in Tuscany*,
2 vols., Eng. ed. New York, *c.* 1924 (excellent illustrations)
R. WITTKOWER, *Architectural Principles in the Age of Humanism*, 3rd
ed., London, 1962
H. WÖLFFLIN, *Renaissance and Baroque*, trans. K. Simon, London, 1964

Painting and Sculpture

G. BRIGANTI, *Italian Mannerism*, London, 1962
S. J. FREEDBERG, *Painting of the High Renaissance...*, 2 vols., Harvard,
1961
C. GOULD, *An Introduction to Italian Renaissance Painting*, London,
1957
J. POPE-HENNESSY, *Italian High Renaissance and Baroque Sculpture*,
3 vols., London, 1963

Monographs

For a fuller list of monographs see P. and L. MURRAY, *Dictionary
of Art and Artists*, London, 1965 (hard-cover edition). The reader
should also consult the British Museum catalogues of Italian drawings: *Michelangelo* by J. WILDE, 1953, and *Raphael and his circle* by
P. POUNCEY and J. GERE, 1962.

Correggio: A. E. POPHAM (on the drawings), London, 1957

Giorgione: G. M. RICHTER, Chicago, 1937; L. COLETTI, London,
1962; L. BALDASS, London, 1965

Lotto: B. BERENSON, London, 1956; P. BIANCONI, London, 1963 (2 vols.)

Michelangelo: C. DE TOLNAY, Princeton, 1943 (in progress; 5 vols. so far), *Art and Thought of Michelangelo*, New York, 1964; L. GOLDSCHEIDER, London, 1953 (complete reproductions); *Letters*, trans. and ed. E. Ramsden, London, 1963, 2 vols.

Raphael: P. OPPÉ, London, 1909; O. FISCHEL, London, 1948, 2 vols.; E. CAMESASCA, London, 1963, 4 vols.

Andrea del Sarto: S. J. FREEDBERG, Harvard, 1963, 2 vols.; J. SHEARMAN, Oxford, 1965, 2 vols.

Titian: H. TIETZE, London, 1950

Acknowledgement

The passage on page 189 from Vasari's *Lives* is reproduced by permission of Penguin Books (trans. George Bull, Penguin Classics, London, 1965)

List of Illustrations

Entries are listed alphabetically under the names of artists. Measurements are given in centimetres, followed by inches. Plate numbers in bold type indicate colour illustrations.

Gesuiti Church, Venice
Photo: Mansell-Alinari   103

TITIAN
Martyrdom of St Lawrence 1564/7
Canvas 175 × 172 (68⅞ × 67¾)
Escorial, Madrid
Photo: Mas   104

TITIAN
Pietà 1573/6
Canvas 350 × 395 (137¾ × 153½)
Accademia, Venice
Photo: Mansell-Alinari   105

TITIAN
Diana and Actaeon 1559

Canvas 190 × 207 (74¾ × 81½)
    Duke of Sutherland Collection,
    on loan to the National Gallery of
    Scotland   140

TITIAN
Tarquin and Lucretia *c.* 1571
Oil 187 × 145 (74⅜ × 57⅛)
    Reproduced by permission of the
    Syndics of the Fitzwilliam Mu-
    seum, Cambridge   **141**

TITIAN
Jacopo Strada 1568
Canvas 125 × 95 (49¼ × 37⅜)
Kunsthistorisches Museum, Vienna
                                142

Index

Praeger World of Art Series

BAROQUE AND ROCOCO ART
GERMAIN BAZIN

EARLY MEDIEVAL ART
JOHN BECKWITH

GREEK ART
JOHN BOARDMAN

ART OF THE ROMANTIC ERA
Romanticism, Classicism, Realism
MARCEL BRION

ANCIENT ARTS OF THE AMERICAS
G. H. S. BUSHNELL

A CONCISE HISTORY OF ENGLISH PAINTING
WILLIAM GAUNT

A CONCISE HISTORY OF PAINTING
From Giotto to Cézanne
MICHAEL LEVEY

ROCOCO TO REVOLUTION
Major Trends in Eighteenth-Century Painting
MICHAEL LEVEY

POP ART
LUCY R. LIPPARD, with contributions by
LAWRENCE ALLOWAY, NANCY MARMER,
and NICOLAS CALAS

THE ART OF THE ANCIENT NEAR EAST
SETON LLOYD

THE IMPRESSIONISTS
FRANÇOIS MATHEY

EUROPEAN SCULPTURE
From Romanesque to Neoclassic
H. D. MOLESWORTH

THE HIGH RENAISSANCE
LINDA MURRAY

THE ART OF THE RENAISSANCE
PETER AND LINDA MURRAY

PREHISTORIC ART
T. G. E. POWELL

A CONCISE HISTORY OF MODERN PAINTING
SIR HERBERT READ

A CONCISE HISTORY OF MODERN SCULPTURE
SIR HERBERT READ

ART OF CHINA, KOREA, AND JAPAN
PETER C. SWANN

ART OF THE BYZANTINE ERA
DAVID TALBOT RICE

ISLAMIC ART
DAVID TALBOT RICE

ANCIENT ARTS OF CENTRAL ASIA
TAMARA TALBOT RICE

A CONCISE HISTORY OF RUSSIAN ART
TAMARA TALBOT RICE

ROMAN ART AND ARCHITECTURE
SIR MORTIMER WHEELER

Praeger World of Art Profiles

CHAGALL
JEAN CASSOU

PICASSO
PIERRE DAIX

VAN GOGH
FRANK ELGAR

HENRY MOORE
SIR HERBERT READ

SEURAT
JOHN RUSSELL

KLEE
GUALTIERI DI SAN LAZZARO